House Beautiful

Instant Inspiration

House Beautiful

Instant Inspiration

Amanda Morrison

EBURY PRESS
LONDON

First published 1994

1 3 5 7 9 10 8 6 4 2

Text and photography
© National Magazine Company Ltd 1994

Amanda Morrison has asserted her right to
be identified as the author of this work.

First published in the United Kingdom
in 1994 by Ebury Press, Random House,
20 Vauxhall Bridge Road, London SW1V 2SA

Random House Australia (Pty) Limited
20 Alfred Street, Milsons Point, Sydney
New South Wales 2061, Australia

Random House New Zealand Limited
18 Poland Road, Glenfield
Auckland 10, New Zealand

Random House South Africa (Pty) Limited
PO Box 337, Bergvlei, South Africa

Random House UK Limited Reg No 954009

A CIP catalogue record for this book is available from
the British Library.

Editor: Gillian Haslam
Design: Terry Jeavons

ISBN 0 091782317

Typeset by Terry Jeavons
Printed in Singapore

Contents

Introduction

RIGHT *Intricately carved wooden fretwork provides an eye-catching focal point in this long, narrow hall.*

A LITTLE INSPIRATION can go a long way, especially when it comes to decorating your home. This book is intended not only to inspire, however, but also to inform. Each chapter is full of bright ideas and useful information. If you've ever wondered where to start tiling the bathroom, or how to make a folding screen or covered headboard, there's a range of step-by-step projects, which will help you to get started.

In the opening chapter the book gives practical advice on how to make the most of colour in your home. There are ideas for devising schemes as well as useful hints on how to compile your own notebooks and swatch cards.

Having introduced colour, the book goes on to cover basic decorating materials from paper and paint to fabric, wood and tiles.

As the quickest means of transforming your home, paint is a popular and versatile medium. Different types of paint and their applications are listed and if you're fascinated by clever paint effects, you'll find recipes for glazes and easy to follow instructions for professional-looking finishes, such a sponging and rag-rolling. If stencilling, however, is more your style there is information on how to achieve the best results and even on how to design and cut your own stencil.

The best ideas are not necessarily the most expensive or time-consuming. Sometimes, just by treating a familiar subject in a new way, you can come up

with a look that is quite unique. In the chapter on paper, for example,

wallpaper borders are given a new lease of life, embellishing shelves or hung

in decorative panels. And even if you can't sew a stitch, you'll find that the

chapter on fabric contains quick and easy ideas for draping and fixing lengths

of muslin in swag holders, making instant tie-backs made from wired lengths

of fake foliage and flowers and how to cheat with curtain clips.

Group several jugs of flowers to create an impact. Here simple dairy milk jugs enhance the glowing purple shades of anemones and hyacinths.

It doesn't matter whether you are a complete novice or an experienced

home decorator – there are ideas and projects to suit everyone. You don't

have to be proficient at DIY to follow some of the ideas in the chapter on

wood and tiles: with a little time and patience, a complete beginner can have

a go at sanding floors or tiling a splashback.

Finally, a chapter on accessories includes hints on hanging pictures and

mirrors for maximum effect, flower arranging for people with little time and

guidance on how to use home fragrance and candlelight to create an

atmosphere which will instantly transform your home.

Whether you are a dab hand with a needle and thread or have never so

much as lifted a paintbrush, I hope that you'll find this book full of inspiring

yet attainable ideas and projects.

Although it might take a little practice before you get the results that you

want, make sure that you have fun trying!

AMANDA MORRISON

Deep raspberry pink walls help to evoke a welcoming atmosphere in this traditional living room, while fresh green foliage and shiny berries add a lively touch.

CHAPTER ONE

Colour

· ·

When it comes to creating an impact, nothing has a more powerful or immediate effect than colour. Impossible to ignore, colour can be used not only to create physical changes but to alter the atmosphere and feel of a room. It touches every aspect of home decorating, from large scale projects like painting an entire room to small decorative details such as cushions and lampshades.

While most people find it quite easy to deal with colour on a small scale, such as choosing their clothes or even the colour of a new car, when it comes to devising colour schemes for their home, they are easily put off by the apparent scale of the task ahead! But there's no more to putting together a colour scheme for your living room than there is to deciding what to wear when you get out of bed in the morning. It's all a matter of confidence, so before you pick up a paint brush or hang the first roll of wallpaper, make sure that you are well-prepared. With so many things to consider, the following guidelines will help by giving advice on how to get started, from the first stage of planning to finding the inspiration. Remember to take your time – by following a few simple steps you can be assured of successful results.

Initial Planning

With all major projects, the success rate depends on the amount of time you spend in planning and preparation. At this stage, planning entails asking yourself some fairly basic questions, not only about colour itself, but also about the function of the room.

This is the time to decide where your priorities lie as far as budget is concerned. Can you afford to re-upholster a tatty three-piece suite, for example, or will you have to come up with another solution?

Practical considerations are of prime importance for most people – so before you set your heart on a pastel-coloured sofa, ask yourself how long it's likely to look as good as new! You may have a brand new home to decorate from scratch or perhaps you've inherited a home or furniture which have to be incorporated into existing schemes. Either way, as colour touches on every aspect of home decorating, putting a colour scheme together involves not only juggling paint swatches but many other things, from carpet and wallpaper samples to tiles and bits of flooring. Different circumstances and rooms will tend to dictate the issues that arise, and there are also some basic points to consider. Think about these before you start and you should be able to anticipate any potential problems before they arise.

Getting To Know Your Room

When you move into a new home, the temptation is to slap up wallpaper and paint as quickly as possible in an attempt to put your own mark on the property. But if you can resist the urge to start redecorating as soon as you set foot inside the door and take time to get to know a room, you'll reap the benefits later.

Before buying a new house, you may have only seen it once or twice at certain times of the day. When you move in, one of the main things that will become apparent is the amount of light a room gets and when it is at its sunniest or dullest. This is not only important when it comes to deciding on colour but may also affect the way you choose to dress the windows and where you position the furniture. And while most people prefer bright rooms, don't worry about those with a chilly aspect – as we'll see later, colour can be used to cheer them up!

Understated shades of ivory and cream help to create a mood of calm in this elegant kitchen/dining room. Wooden flooring and accessories lend warmth to the scheme, without detracting from its neutral tones.

The function of a room will also influence your decisions: a living room should be comfortable, a kitchen practical and a hallway welcoming. The amount of time you spend in any one room may also influence the way that you decorate it. Bathrooms and dining rooms, for example, lend themselves to more experimental ideas and dramatic colours as it's unlikely that you'll spend a great deal of time in these areas. It's probably true to say, on the other hand, that you'd be unwilling to put your most daring colour scheme to the test in a bedroom.

The way that you and your family use a room – where you like to sit, which kitchen lay-outs suits you best, etc. – will soon become apparent after you have spent a little time getting to know your new home. That, too, is likely to affect your decorating decisions.

Finding The Inspiration

Half the fun in planning a new look for any room is collecting all sorts of pictures and swatches that inspire you. Top designers use this ploy when they are devising schemes or forecasting trends in colour, pattern and texture, so why not take a leaf out of their book? Amassing anything from magazine cuttings, paint swatches and fabric samples to picture postcards and pieces of wallpaper will prove invaluable in helping you to form a definite idea of the look you want to create. This sort of collection will help you to decide on not only the actual materials you wish to incorporate, but also on overall atmosphere or style.

Keep any such bits and pieces in a notebook that you can carry around in your pocket or bag for easy reference. And when browsing around showrooms and shops, don't be afraid to ask for small samples of wallpaper and fabric which you can add to your 'ideas book'. Eventually this will form an 'at a glance' reference as well as acting as a stepping stone to the next stage of planning – compiling your own Designer Swatch Card (see page 24).

Deciding On a Starting Point

In many respects, redecorating a familiar room in an existing home is a great deal easier than starting from scratch in a brand new house. Whichever you are faced with, deciding on a starting point around which to base your colour scheme is vital. But just how do you go about selecting a good starting point?

The starting point is likely to be something that you will have to live with for many years so should be looked on as an investment. Bearing this in mind, therefore, it's better to base your colour scheme around a major purchase such as a carpet, sofa or curtains which will be expensive to replace. There are some commonsense guidelines to help you decide on where to start.

- Remember the scale of the room and be careful that you don't choose anything with proportions that will overpower it.

- Work out how you are going to combine old items of furniture with new things.

- Consider the balance of patterned and plain areas. It doesn't matter whether you choose an elaborate paisley patterned sofa or a pair of plain curtains as a starting point for your colour scheme as long as you see them in the context of the finished room.

- Consider the practicalities. If you are determined to have a pale, peachy-coloured living room, it's wiser to use paint, paper or curtains to create the effect rather than rely on upholstery or carpets which are unlikely to remain in a spotless condition for very long.

- Make sure that the chosen item is not going to restrict you to one look or scheme when you want to redecorate at a later date.

- Above all, make sure that you really like it. After all, you are going to have to live with it for years to come.

The key things to remember are:

- Spend time planning.
- If you can, live with a room for a while before deciding on how to decorate.
- Keep a scrapbook of magazine cuttings, postcards, swatches and samples to help you make a final choice.
- Work out what you want to (or have to) use as a starting point.
- Consider the balance of patterned and plain areas.
- Decide on the atmosphere that you want to create – a restful bedroom, a stimulating dining room or welcoming hallway, for example.

But even when armed with all this advice, the swatches and samples, how do you translate the information you have amassed into a fully decorated room?

Decorated in restrained shades of cream, this narrow corridor becomes a surprisingly light and airy space. Large pots of ferns introduce a vivid splash of colour.

How To Choose Colours

Just like the fashion industry, colours in home decorating tend to go through cycles of being 'in ' or 'out'. But unlike fashion, these cycles move slowly so you are likely to see the same shades and themes for years rather than months. Trends will obviously influence any choices you make, partly by affecting your taste and partly by dictating what is available in shops. The trick is to learn how to combine classic styles and colours that you really like and which never date with more contemporary colours, patterns and accessories.

Before getting down to the task of co-ordinating different colours, patterns and textures, you must ask yourself what kind of atmosphere you are hoping to achieve. It is well known that various colours and shades can have a dramatic effect on our moods and nowhere is this more evident than in your own home. If you've ever walked into a house and found it unwelcoming or depressing, it may well be due to the choice of colour.

The following guide will give you an idea of the best colours to use in particular rooms but it isn't an inflexible set of rules. Much of it is just common sense and if it sounds familiar, it is probably because it echoes your own instinctive reaction to certain colours and shades.

White
Perfect for creating an air of space, white does not impose a mood. It provides a great background for showing off paintings or other works of art, but from a practical point of view, white will show every speck of dirt so, for families with children or pets, it is probably best avoided!

Cream
A standard safe choice, shades of cream and ivory are unlikely to offend but used alone are a touch uninspiring. Like white, however, they make a good background for

paintings and interesting accessories like richly patterned kelims. A touch of warmth prevents these shades from having the same clinical feel as white.

Red

A stimulating and exciting colour, red also has the power to overwhelm. Useful in areas where you need to feel alert but beware if you are the kind of person who tires easily or feels claustrophobic. Try using small quantities of red for its energizing power.

Orange

A warm and friendly colour which will help to create a cheerful and welcoming atmosphere, but which should be avoided in bedrooms or if you are feeling under stress.

By limiting the basic colour scheme, you'll find it easy to combine several different patterns. Here stripes, florals and plaids in rich wine shades work well together.

Pink

A popular choice for bedrooms, pink evokes passion and caring. Too cool a shade of pink is liable to sap your level of energy so it is best to stick to warmer tones.

Yellow

Generally perceived as being a bright and optimistic colour, yellow is a good choice if you are feeling depressed or sluggish but, unless used in its subtlest shades, it can be an unsettling choice for a bedroom.

Green

A fresh and clean colour, although cooler shades can appear rather sterile. Green is generally accepted as a calming colour so is a good choice if you are liable to stress. However, if you are feeling withdrawn or lethargic, green will only accentuate those emotions.

Turquoise

Combines the complementary qualities of soothing and energizing. A versatile colour that can be used to good effect throughout your home. Unlike pure shades of blue and green which often seem too calming, turquoise is a well balanced colour that aids positive relaxation.

Blue

Chosen by conformists and those who prefer to stick with convention, blue, like green, has a very soothing effect. Its relaxing qualities make it ideal for evoking an air of calm but in living and dining areas, blue lends an air of detachment which is liable to make you feel uncomfortable.

Violet

Spiritual and meditative, shades of violet are best avoided by those with a tendency to daydream! Richer shades of purple, however, are perfect for creating a rich and festive feel.

Magenta

A peaceful and dignified choice, magenta represents contentment so should be avoided by those who may feel tempted to opt out or 'sit on the fence' for the rest of their days.

Black

Chosen by the self-assured who are successful and feel in control of their lives, black is something of a status colour and should be avoided by those who feel at all anxious or nervous!

Grey

Like black, dark shades of grey express achievement while light grey demonstrates a need for acceptance. Should be avoided as the main component in a colour scheme, and used instead as a secondary player. Most effective when tinted with a subtle blue, green or pink.

FAR LEFT *Buttercup yellow and primary red are an unfailingly cheerful partnership. Walls painted a subtle shade of yellow provide a sunny background without detracting from the brightly coloured furnishings.*

LEFT *Blue-green shades are particularly appropriate for bathrooms. Subtle layers of paint have been colourwashed on to the walls, emphasizing the aquatic atmosphere.*

COLOUR COMBINATIONS

When browsing through pattern books and colour charts most people find it easy to identify individual colours that they like. The problems start when those shades have to be used with other colours or incorporated into an existing scheme. Whether you decide to play it safe by using different shades of the same colour or want to create something a bit more dynamic with strong contrasts, clever combinations are the key to making colour work for you.

USING THE SAME SHADES AND TONES

Rooms which are decorated in a single colour don't have to look uninspired. By using varying shades you can build up an elegant yet understated scheme. Subtle differences in shade may be used to delineate different areas such as woodwork, windows or walls, and there's certainly no shortage of materials. From delicately tinted paints to wood stains, fabric and flooring, you can make a selection that, though similar in colour, offers interesting textural differences. This play of contrasting textures is an important, if often neglected, aspect of putting together a colour scheme and may be used to create interesting effects. Contrasting textures add depth and variety; and in single shade rooms particularly they help to prevent the scheme from appearing bland and two-dimensional.

If you feel a little apprehensive about devising your own scheme, it's often easiest to start with different shades of a single colour. That could mean anything from a naturally inspired ivory and taupe scheme or a feminine mix of different shades of pink.

With such a versatile background, you'll find it easy to change the appearance of the rooms simply by changing the accessories. Everything from elegant fabrics to richly-patterned kelims work well against these understated tones.

WARM AND COOL COLOURS

Complementary colours are those that sit opposite one another on the colour wheel and include pairs such as orange and turquoise; red and green and yellow and blue. The merest touch of a complementary colour is an invaluable way of adding vitality to lacklustre schemes, although if used in equal proportions, they tend to produce a far from harmonious effect. While the contrast of rich, warm colours and cool citrus shades is an exciting recipe, it's important that you consider a couple of points – intensity and proportion – before you start.

The intensity (or depth) of a colour gives it its strength. If you plan to use two complementary colours of the same intensity, make sure that you don't use them in equal proportions. A fifty-fifty balance like this would mean that each colour had equal power and would result in an unpleasant clash!

If you wish to use similar proportions, make sure that you alter the intensity of each complementary colour. Given equal billing, pillar box red and emerald green would clash horribly; yet dark pine green looks wonderful against a weathered pink background and the same two basic colours provide the basis for the successful scheme. Juxtaposed in their most intense form, complementary colours have a dramatic effect which has far more impact when the colours are used in different proportions.

- Use paint charts and small test pots to experiment with the effects that can be achieved with different quantities and intensities of colour.

- If you are having difficulty finding inspiration, many fabric and wallpaper designs incorporate both warm and cool shades and are therefore useful starting points.

- Using just two complementary colours as a basis for a scheme is not as limiting as you might think. By adjusting the strength and proportions, you can come up with a wide range of effects.

- Experiment with accessories to help you gain confidence combining warm and cool shades. Even the smallest details – a red plate against a green tablecloth or a verdigris bowl containing oranges – can look stunning.

- Some of the best-loved and most successful colour partnerships are based on complementary shades – yellow and blue or terracotta and navy, for example.

A bright fruit bowl appears as an oasis of colour in this black and white living room. You don't have to decorate an entire area like this though – black and white works just as well in small areas such as a tiled hall floor.

BLACK AND WHITE

The dramatic effect created by these two opposites certainly packs a punch. While most people prefer to use black and white with restraint (in chequerboard floors, for example), for those with a taste for adventure, the combination offers tremendous scope for imaginative interiors.

The way that you balance the two shades is vitally important and will affect the mood of the room. While large areas such as walls tend to be predominantly white, darker tones can be introduced with printed fabrics and other accessories. And the benefit of working with such a limited palette is that it is easy to mix different patterns and textures: linked by a common colour theme, materials as diverse as vinyl flooring, ceramic wall tiles and Toile de Jouy fabric work well together. If you are unhappy with a black and white scheme, a simple adjustment of the proportions will often solve the problem.

- While its graphic qualities appeal to lovers of contemporary design, black and white makes a surprisingly good background for older furniture, too.
- Black and white flooring is both practical and versatile which makes it an ideal choice for using throughout small flats and houses.
- If you like black and white but find the combination a little too stark for your taste, add brightly-coloured accessories such as vases or lampshades.
- Small spaces look particularly effective when decorated in black and white so it is ideal for hallways and loos.

Pattern and Texture

Of course, when you are putting together a colour scheme, it's not only colour itself that you have to consider. Pattern and texture both have important roles to play. As already mentioned, texture may be used to great effect in rooms decorated in different shades of one colour. These understated schemes allow the eye to concentrate on fine details.

By sticking to a limited palette, you'll be able to mix several different patterns, too. Look through the photographs of co-ordinated ranges of wallpaper and fabric to get ideas for decorating your own home with a variety of patterns.

- Mix floral prints with smart checks and stripes for a contemporary look that has classic appeal.
- Remember to consider the scale of a print as well as its design.
- Cushions, lampshades and other accessories can completely alter the mood of a room and are ideal ways of introducing pattern.

One Room, Two Ways

The colour of a room can completely change it character as well as its appearance. Here, the same small room has been given two quite different treatments using an interesting range of materials and ideas. Both schemes rely on limited palettes but have two quite distinctive looks.

LIGHT ROOM

- Neutral tones help you to make the most of an interesting range of textures as diverse as sisal flooring and crewel-work curtains.
- Unexpected combinations work well within a subtle range of shades: a marble fireplace looks quite at home with more rustic materials such as wrought iron and wood.
- Several different patterns have been successfully mixed in this room: from the damask-covered sofa to checked cushions and patterned wallpaper.
- Bleached wooden flooring could be continued into other rooms that lead from this one to create an impression of continuing space.
- Although the accessories used here continue the natural theme, they could equally well have been chosen for contrast and are a good way of introducing a second colour.

DARK ROOM

- Lighting is particularly important in dark rooms. Wall-mounted and side lamps are a more effective way of creating atmosphere and can be used to highlight specific areas.
- A navy Roman blind edged in gold damask is a smart alternative to curtains and hardly reduces the light.
- If you cannot afford to re-upholster a sofa to co-ordinate with your new scheme, a simple throw works wonders as a temporary measure. This plaid throw has tones of navy and gold but also introduces shades of pink and white.
- This predominantly navy room has touches of complementary golden yellow for contrast and warmth.

Designer Tips For Colour Scheming

- A simple recipe for success is to use several shades of one colour in a room, eg pale green walls with darker green woodwork.
- Stick two basic colours in any one scheme/room. You can add further colours with accessories like lampshades and cushions.
- Remember that colours can create a warm or cool atmosphere so it's best to steer clear of cold shades of blue and green in north-facing rooms.
- The same colour or shade used throughout a room or other area, whether as painted walls or carpeting, will create the impression of space.

- If you are nervous about using colour, start with a neutral shade (like cream or white tinted with colour) and add a stronger colour such as blue or green. Just be careful that the room doesn't appear too cold or uninviting.
- Decide on a starting point for your scheme and keep referring back to it when you are deciding on anything from lighting to paint colour.

Above all, however, colour is a matter of personal taste. Although there are guidelines to help you devise your own colour schemes, they are only to help get you started. Once you gain confidence, you'll find that there are no true rights and wrongs and that rules are made to be broken!

BELOW *Whether you choose light or dark shades to decorate a room, subtle nuances of colour and texture are the keys to enlivening your scheme.*

Designer Swatch Cards

Once you've done your initial planning, you will want to assemble samples and swatches on one page so that you can see at a glance all the necessary elements that make up a well-designed interior. The following pages contain all the information that you'll need when you are planning to redecorate your home. Simply photocopy a set of swatch cards and keep them in a plastic folder that you can carry around with you for easy reference.

The grid should be used for mapping out a rough outline of the room that you are working on, with details such as ceiling heights, the direction that doors open and

From picture postcards to magazine cuttings and fabric samples, inspiration may be found in a diverse range of sources.

any immovable features such as fireplaces and radiators noted. In addition to this information, it's a good idea to take a snapshot of the room which you can clip onto the grid. You'll find this helps you to picture fabrics, paints and wallcoverings in situ when you are out looking at samples. There are also spaces for you to attach wallpaper and paint swatches as well as areas for upholstery fabrics, wallpaper borders and flooring. You may not need to use all the space or you might find that you need more – just adapt the cards to suit your own needs.

Remember to keep a note of design names and reference numbers as these will be crucial when it comes to ordering. You should also take down any other information you feel is relevant – the name of the manufacturer, fabric width and pattern repeat, the shop(s) or showroom(s) that you visited and, of course, prices. Armed with these details you should be able to work out roughly the amount of material you'll need to and how much it is liable to cost. This information is invaluable not only when you are planning a room, but can be useful later on if for any reason you need to replace anything.

Finally there are a couple of window outlines – one for curtains with a track mounted above the frame and one for a recessed blind – where you can note dimensions, quantities and any other useful information. There's room for extra notes and a chart to help you convert imperial to metric and vice versa (remember to take a calculator with you when shopping).

swatch points

- Check that all wallpaper rolls display the same batch number to ensure correct colour matching. Buy a spare roll to patch any worn areas in the future.
- Samples of tiles will be too heavy to attach to your swatch card. Carry them separately or attach a sample of a matching paint colour as a rough guide.
- The scale used in this grid is one square to 10 cm (4 in) but create your own scale to suit the size of the room.
- When choosing upholstery fabrics, make sure they meet fire retardancy regulations – check with your retailer.
- Staple (rather than stick) your swatches in the relevant boxes so that you can flip them up to read the details underneath each one.
- Without moving from your chair, you can work out how best to position bulky items of furniture by using paper cut-out scale models against the grid.

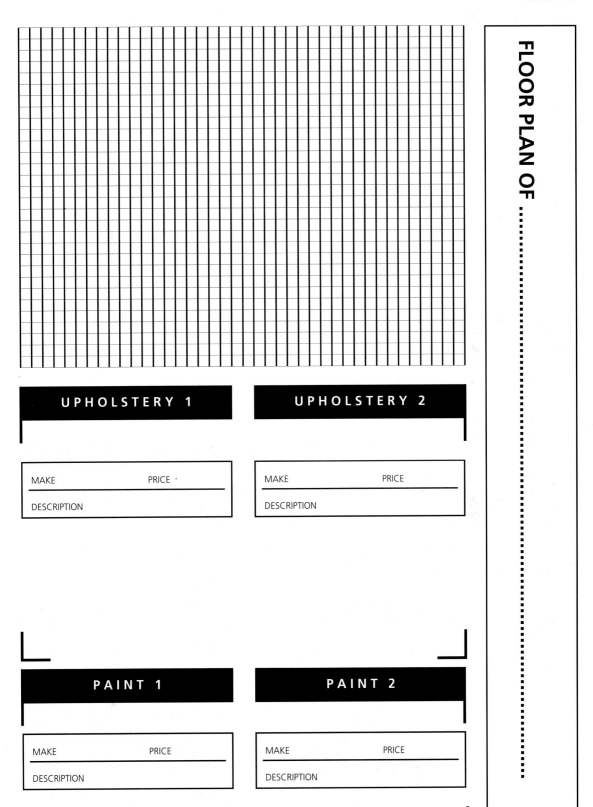

FLOOR PLAN OF ....

UPHOLSTERY 1

MAKE   PRICE ·

DESCRIPTION

UPHOLSTERY 2

MAKE   PRICE

DESCRIPTION

PAINT 1

MAKE   PRICE

DESCRIPTION

PAINT 2

MAKE   PRICE

DESCRIPTION

WALLPAPER 1

MAKE	PRICE
DESCRIPTION	

WALLPAPER 2

MAKE	PRICE
DESCRIPTION	

BORDER

MAKE	PRICE
DESCRIPTION	

FLOORING

MAKE	PRICE
DESCRIPTION	

NOTES

CURTAINS

* TOTAL MATERIAL REQUIRED

METRES   YARDS

LINING   TIE-BACKS

BLINDS

* TOTAL MATERIAL REQUIRED

METRES   YARDS

LINING   TIE-BACKS

TRACK

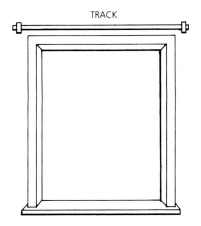

TRACK

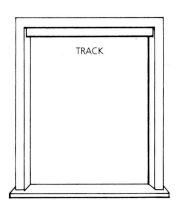

* To calculate amount of fabric required for curtains or blinds you will first need to measure up accurately. Make sure you select the correct type of heading tape or blind kit. Consult a good retailer before buying.

CONVERTING MEASUREMENTS
FEET TO CENTIMETRES – multiply by 30.48
CENTIMETRES TO FEET – divide by 30.48
YARDS TO METRES – multiply by 0.9144
METRES TO YARDS – divide by 0.9144

Metric	5 mm	1 cm	2.5 cm	5 cm	7 cm	10 cm	12 cm	15 cm	18 cm	20 cm	23 cm	25 cm	28 cm	30 cm	91 cm	1 m	3.05 m
Imperial	1/4 in	1/2 in	1 in	2 in	3 in	4 in	5 in	6 in	7 in	8 in	9 in	10 in	11 in	12 in (1ft)	36 in	39 in	10 ft

CHAPTER TWO

Paint

If colour is the very essence of instant impact, paint provides the easiest and most immediate method of application. And given the many different types of paint around, virtually any surface in your home, from walls to woodwork, metal to melamine, can be treated successfully.

The beauty of paint is its versatility. While it is an ideal medium for covering vast areas of wall, it may also, using the correct technique and brush, be applied in intricate detail. It also offers the best choice of colour of all media. While you may strike lucky and find an ideal match in wallpaper or fabric, it's far more likely that you'll do so on a paint colour chart. While the range of colours available will vary according to the type of paint you need, these days most large paint manufacturers offer a service where more unusual or subtle shades may be mixed to order according to a 'recipe' of more basic colours which gives you an even greater choice. So when you are devising a colour scheme, it's best to start with fabric, carpet or wallpaper and then find a shade of paint that you like.

As well as being a relatively inexpensive material for home decorating, paint is easy to work with and requires no specialist skills. Preparation, patience and common sense are all that's required to prevent potential calamities such as dripping, shading or smudging. And once you have mastered the basics, the potential is there to experiment with more sophisticated paint techniques such as stencilling, rag rolling and dragging. Even these seemingly complicated finishes, however, are not difficult to learn. All that's required is a free afternoon, some pots of paint and a little patience!

There are a great number of different paints on the market but whatever manufacturers choose to call them, they fall into two distinct categories – oil or water-based. Oil paints are soluble with white spirit while water-based paints are, of course, soluble with water.

Liquid gloss
Has a hard, shiny finish and requires an undercoat. Seal wooden surfaces with a primer before applying (a combined primer and undercoat will save on drying time). Mainly used for wood and metal (eg radiators). Coverage per litre is around 17 square metres.

Non-drip gloss
Has a high-shine finish and its gel-like texture means that it will not drip or run. Though it does not require an undercoat, bare wood should be primed. Mainly use for wood, metal and plastic surfaces, such as drainpipes. Coverage per litre is around 12-15 square metres.

Self-undercoating gloss
Combines the qualities of liquid and non-drip gloss. Has a thick, creamy consistency and dries to a high-shine finish. Covers most colours with a single coat. Mainly used for wood, metal and plastic. Coverage per litre is around 10 square metres.

Mid-sheen oil-based paints
Soft-sheen finish. Though less tough than gloss paint and harder to keep clean, it does not require an undercoat. Two or more coats usually required. Bare wood should be

primed first. Commonly known as 'eggshell', it can be used on walls or as a subtle alternative to gloss for woodwork or metal. Coverage per litre is around 16 square metres.

Vinyl silk emulsion

Has a silky low-sheen finish and does not require an undercoat. Ideal for damp walls in steamy areas, such as kitchens and bathrooms, and is easy to wipe clean. Silky finish is liable to emphasise flaws but it is good for highlighting relief patterned wallpapers, such as Anaglypta. Mainly used on walls and ceilings. Coverage per litre is around 13-14 square metres.

Vinyl matt emulsion

Has a soft, matt finish and does not require an undercoat. The most popular choice for walls and ceilings. Helps to disguise uneven surfaces. Coverage per litre is around 14-15 square metres.

Solid emulsion/roller paint

Is available in either matt or silk finish and does not require an undercoat. Comes packaged ready to use in a paint tray but has a fairly limited range of colours. Use on walls and ideal for ceilings as its thick texture means that it will not drip or run. Coverage per litre is around 12 square metres.

Painting a Room

Whether you are working with a paint brush or roller, the same basic rules apply when painting a room.

- Start with the ceiling, then paint the walls, window frames, doors, mouldings (such as dado rails and cornice) and finally, skirting boards.
- Always work away from the natural light source.
- When painting walls, start in the top right corner and work down the wall to the bottom right, covering areas of about 75

square cm (2 square feet) at a time. Go on to the next top section and carry on working in vertical strips until the wall is complete. (If you are left-handed, start at the top left corner.)

- If you need a break, try to make sure that you stop at a corner rather than mid-wall to avoid shading.
- Paint edges along skirting boards and corners with a small brush before you start on the main section of wall.

Once you have got to grips with the basics of painting, you will find that a wide range of special effects are easy to achieve.

Stencilling

Stencilling has enjoyed a long and varied history and is now one of the most popular forms of home decorating. This is partly because it is a relatively quick and easy way of injecting decorative interest, partly because it is inexpensive, and partly because of the tremendous choice of designs available. Whether you are inspired by the charming rustic patterns so beloved by the American settlers or prefer elegant architectural friezes, you can be sure to find a readymade stencil for the job. And although there are specialist paints and paint sticks devised specifically for stencilling, you can also use emulsion, spray paint or fabric paint to great effect.

If you have never tried your hand at stencilling, its best to start with a ready-cut design and work on something that is a manageable scale, such as a tray or small table top. Ready-cut stencils are widely available and are usually made from waxed card or plastic. Stencils may be used as single motifs, repeat patterns (for covering the entire surface of a wall, for example) or in a continuous line to create stylish, decorative borders.

The joy of stencilling is that, once you have mastered the basics, it's easy to make your own designs. Using fabric, tiles or even patterned crockery as inspiration, you can lift a section of the design, simplify it and transfer it to a stencil. This will then allow you to draw various elements of a room, such as curtains and lampshades, together with a stencilled border.

Making Your Own Stencil

You don't have to be a master craftsman to achieve professional results. Providing you follow this basic guide and take your time, you can create a unique look for your home.

you will need

- Tracing paper
- Felt-tip and ball-point pens
- Chalk
- Oiled manila card
- Cutting board (an old vinyl or lino tile will suffice perfectly)
- Scalpel
- Masking tape

Preparation

While stencilling is suitable for most surfaces, ceramic tiles, vinyl, glass and other shiny non-porous surfaces can prove tricky and should only be attempted once you are practised. Any surfaces that you work on should be clean, dry and free from dust or grease. Ensure that your design will fit the area to be stencilled by measuring before you start and then having a practice run on a scrap of paper or card. If you aren't too sure how a design will look, stencil a rough version in your chosen colours and pin it in place to give you an idea of how the finished design will look in situ.

Once you have decided on your design, transfer it on to the manila card. You can do this in two ways:

step by step
MAKING A STENCIL

1. Trace out the pattern onto the tracing paper in black felt-tip pen. Then chalk the back of the tracing paper and lay it on to the card, chalky side down. Draw over the pattern again, this time with a hard pencil or ball-point pen. Remove the trace and draw in the design with felt-tip pen, blocking in the areas to be cut out.

OR

Use a grid system and map out the pattern freehand. Again, block in the areas to be cut out.

2. Carefully cut out the shaded areas with a scalpel. Always draw the scalpel towards you, moving the card as necessary, but work slowly – a slip of a scalpel can not only damage your stencil but is liable to give you a very nasty cut. If you make a minor slip when cutting, use a thin strip of of masking tape to seal the card on either side.

BELOW *Stencils inspired by classical designs have been used both above and below the dado rail. The fan-like motif is particularly effective at breaking up the distressed ochre paint finish.*

step by step
STENCILLING

1. Position the stencil on the surface that you want to decorate. Keep it in place with spray mount, pins or masking tape.

2. Pour a small amount of paint into a saucer or other small container. Dip your stencil brush in and dab off any excess paint on a piece of scrap paper – the key to successful stencilling is working with a very dry brush.

3. Holding the brush like a pencil, use light circular movements. Stencil outside edges first before moving towards the centre.

4. Gently lift the stencil when all areas have been coloured. Check the stencil for a build-up of paint and wipe off if necessary.

5. Reposition the stencil using the register marks if using a ready-cut stencil (as shown here) or measure accordingly. Fix in place and continue as before.

6. Here a dual colour pattern is being used. When you start the second colour, position the stencil over the first colourway and, ideally using a different brush, apply the second colour. (Paints produced for stencilling are fast-drying, allowing the whole process to be completed relatively quickly.)

7. To create more depth of colour, you can add shading to your design once the base colours have dried. For example, a fruit design can be made to look more realistic by adding a second colour as a highlight on the curve of the fruit.

8. To stencil a corner, draw a line at 45 degrees to the corner in pencil. Fix masking tape along one side of the line. Stencil the other side, continuing the pattern up and on to the tape. Move tape to the other side of the line and stencil as above. Remove tape and erase pencil line.

Paint Finishes

Paint can also be used to create many different decorative effects which are easy to master yet which give a professional finish to bare walls or other surfaces. Very little in the way of specialist materials is required and, with a bit of practice on a spare piece of card or off-cut of wood, you'll find that you are ready to progress on to relatively large-scale projects. There's no great mystery attached to achieving a wide range of finishes – all you need is ordinary paint, time and patience! After a while, you may even want to have a go at devising your own tailor-made paint effects.

- A thin glaze of colour either washed or sponged on to a wall is an instant and effective way of toning down too bright a colour. Try shades of terracotta or rust against bright yellow or inky blue against emerald green.

- Always test colours on a scrap piece of card or wood as colour combinations do not always turn out quite as you would expect!

- Popular in Georgian times, dragging is a subtle way of emphasising the height of a room and has a more formal appeal than most other paint finishes.

- Remember you can have too much of a good thing. If you intend using more than one paint finish in a room, make sure that they are compatible and will not detract from one another, for example a subtle dragging or sponging with a more dramatic finish is acceptable while two powerful effects like marbling and combing will just look a mess.

- If your walls are in poor condition, the unevenly blended shades of many paint finishes help to disguise the imperfections.

- If you are a complete beginner, start with a relatively simple effect such as ragging or sponging and progress on to more complicated finishes like marbling as you become more accomplished.

- Decide on the area you want to treat – it may be a wall, a door or a piece of furniture. Gather together all the equipment you will need so you won't be interrupted.

GLAZED LOOKS

Glaze is the medium that you work with to create paint effects. Depending on the effect that you want, you can apply the glaze to a prepared surface with a medium like a rag or sponge which will instantly give a textured appearance. Alternatively the glaze may be brushed on and then worked before it dries.

There are two types of glaze – oil glaze and emulsion glaze.

Oil glaze is applied over a base coat to give it a top layer of transparent colour. This type of glaze can only be applied on top of eggshell or vinyl silk paint. Mix oil glaze in the following proportions: one part of coloured eggshell paint, two parts of oil glaze, 150 ml (1/4 pint) of white spirit. Mix the paint with a little white spirit so that it will disperse evenly when added to the glaze. Finally, you could add a couple of teaspoons of white eggshell paint to mellow the glaze.

Oil glaze is very easy to work with as it dries slowly and any mistakes can simply be wiped off with a drop of white spirit on a rag. When the glaze is dry, protect it with two coats of matt or eggshell lacquer, preferably not polyurethane as this has a yellow tinge.

Emulsion glaze is made from matt emulsion paint with added water. A good ratio is 550ml of water to one litre of emulsion paint. Alternatively, use up leftover emulsion by tinting it to the shade you want with any water soluble colouring agent, such as artists' acrylic colours or PVA colours. Blend the colour with water before adding to the glaze. Emulsion glaze can only be used on walls painted with matt emulsion.

SPATTERING

This method gives a look that resembles the finely textured surface of granite or stone. Load your brush with diluted emulsion paint, taking care to wipe the excess off against a hard rim. Then gently run your finger across the bristles to release a fine spray of paint droplets on to the wall. Stiffer brushes – you could even try using a toothbrush – are better for spattering than softer varieties and if you don't want to use your finger, the handle of a small paint brush or an artist's palette knife make good substitutes. Use two or three different colours to build up a rich yet subtle surface.

COMBING

One of the more dramatic paint effects, combing is remarkably easy. As its name suggests, all that's involved is drawing a home-made cardboard comb or a decorator's metal or rubber comb through wet glaze. The striking result is often used in conjunction with plain areas. Combing is a popular method of decorating furniture, floors and doors.

COLOUR-WASHING

A very soft and delicate finish, reminiscent of watercolour painting, colour-washing is achieved by using a large brush to paint overlapping arcs of colour on to the wall. Once dry, the effect is repeated several times until there is a build-up of four or five layers. You can blend any hard edges with a large brush before the glaze has dried thoroughly.

STIPPLING

A gently mottled effect which makes an excellent background for hanging pictures, mirrors and prints. First, paint glaze on to the prepared surface in a strip no wider then 1 metre (1 yard). Then, with a stippling brush, press into the wet glaze to break up the surface, taking care to clean the brush frequently as it is liable to become clogged with glaze.

DRAGGING

A finely striped finish which has an understated, elegant look. First, paint glaze on to the wall then, holding a long bristled brush almost flat (ie almost parallel to the wall) draw it down through the glaze in a single, even stroke to create distinctive subtle stripes.

Sponged in delicate shades of peach and cream, this wall has a subtly textured appearance which is emphasized by the glow of lamplight.

SPONGING

If you are a beginner, the technique of sponging is not only straightforward but creates a delicate and attractive pattern. Make sure that you use a natural sea sponge as the irregular holes and soft texture give the best results. Man-made sponges can be used but they will give a much harsher effect which has a totally different feel from that created by a natural sponge.

If you are working with oil glaze, you have the option of sponging on or sponging off. As this suggests, the texture is created either by applying the glaze directly on to a prepared surface with the sponge itself, or by painting on the glaze with a brush and then using the sponge to 'lift' off areas so creating a negative sponged effect. This positive and negative aspect of paint effects only applies to oil glaze which remains in a workable state for some time after its application. If you are using emulsion glaze, you will only be able to sponge on as the glaze will dry too quickly for sponging off to be effective.

step by step
SPONGING

1. Start with the wall which has the smallest area so that you are able to build up your confidence gradually. One wall should be completed at a session, but don't be daunted by that: it's very quick work!

2. To sponge on, first wet the sponge and then squeeze all the water out to expand it to its full size. Dip the sponge into the glaze and then blot it on a piece of spare absorbent paper. This will not only help to distribute the glaze evenly over the sponge, it also prevents any blobs or runs from appearing in the final pattern.

3. To apply the glaze, hold the sponge at arm's length and dab it very gently on to the wall. Dot the sponge about so that the imprints you make are random and look natural. The more lightly you work, the more delicate and lacy the pattern will be. Recharge the sponge whenever the pattern is beginning to get faint – and remember to blot it each time.

4. You shouldn't aim to cover the ground coat completely with sponging – some of the base colour should always show through the glaze. Work across the whole wall at once, leaving gaps which you can go back to later to fill.

5. For a richer effect, you could leave the glaze to dry before mixing a deeper tone (or even another colour) and use that to fill the gaps.

RAGGING

As its name suggests, ragging involves using a scrunched up piece of fabric to apply (or remove) glaze. The type of effect that you achieve will depend on the sort of fabric you use, so it's well worth experimenting with everything from muslin to old T shirts! Heavy cottons tend to give a fairly crisp pattern while chamois leather is good if you want a strong finish. You could even substitute a plastic bag for fabric for a fun alternative which will have its own distinct look. As patterns can be striking, it's best to aim for a glaze that does not contrast severely with the base coat.

Once you have mastered these finishes, you might even like to have a go devising your own paint effects. There are specialist books and kits available which have information on more complicated effects such as verdigris, crackle glaze, marble and tortoiseshell.

step by step
RAGGING

1. *To start, bunch up the rag in the palm of your hand and dip it into the glaze. Blot the excess glaze on a spare piece of paper, at the same time noting the effect of the pattern.*

2. *Press the rag lightly on to the surface of the wall, turning your hand and re-bunching the rag from time to time so that the resulting pattern is varied. When the rag becomes clogged with paint and is unworkable, it's time to change it.*

If you are using oil glaze, you can also use scraps of fabric for ragging off. Don't try this with emulsion glaze as it dries too quickly.

3. *To rag off, apply glaze to the wall in a strip no wider than 1 metre (1 yard). Press the bunched up rag into the glazed surface and make a pattern by taking off some of the glaze. The pattern will become more indistinct the more often you dab with the rag.*

4. *You can also shape the fabric into a sausage shape and, with a hand at either end, roll it up and down the wall to create yet another variation on the ragging theme.*

You can create a wide range of effects with rag rolling. The end result depends not only on your choice of colour but on the type of fabric used.

Make a grand entrance by painting a stunning chequerboard floor. Deep pine green and sunny yellow make a change from more conventional colour combinations.

Painted Chequerboard Floor

Who said paint could only be used on walls and woodwork? This striking floor would look welcoming in a hallway or smart kitchen. It involves no special skills though you will need to spend some time in preparation before you start. Remember that the more varnish you apply, the more hard-wearing the floor will be.

You can either use two contrasting colours as shown here, or two toning shades for a more subtle effect. See the instructions in step 4 for testing different colours. For a co-ordinated scheme, pick up colours used on the walls, in curtains or upholstery. Alternate black and white diamonds would be ideal for a modern, sophisticated look.

Before you start

Before you start trying anything on the floor, you must make a floor plan by drawing a scale version of your floor on squared paper, mapping out the design you want. It may seem time-consuming, but could save costly mistakes later. Remember to follow the instructions in step 5 for preparing the floor surface before painting.

you will need

- Squared paper
- Floor primer
- Roller or large paint brush
- Vinyl matt emulsion
- Large piece of card
- Ruler
- Set square
- String
- Drawing pins
- Pencil
- Rubber
- Straight edge
- Scissors
- Masking tape
- 4cm (1 1/2 in) paint brushes
- Varnish

PAINTED CHEQUERBOARD FLOOR

1. *Allow one square of paper to 30cm (12in) of room. If your room has too many alcoves or fitted furniture to make a wall-to-wall rectangle possible, consider a plain border of 7.5-13cm (3-5in). Remember, however, that the aim of a painted floor is not rigid perfection – that's what vinyl flooring is for! So if some of your squares end up slightly larger than others, or not quite at right angles, it doesn't matter. If, like this example, the room is an awkward shape opt for a basic rectangle within the floor space.*

2. *Next, work out the size of your pattern. The diamond shapes here have a 46cm (18in) diagonal (see figure 1) as this divided exactly into the dimensions of the room – 3.2 x 3.7m (126 x 144in).*

3. *Draw two diagonal lines from the corners of your room plan or rectangle to find the dead centre. Starting from here, draw your chequerboard design. If you want a diamond dead centre, which means two half diamonds at either edge of the room, draw your first diamond either side of the central point (see figure 2). If you want a line of complete diamonds going across the room, draw your first one to one side of the centre point (see figure 3). The diamonds in this example are quite large. For a busier pattern – and more work – halve the diagonal measurement. Few houses have perfectly straight walls, but that doesn't have to be a problem – just cheat a little! If you simply run on your final diamonds up to the skirting board no one will notice when the room is in use (see figure 4).*

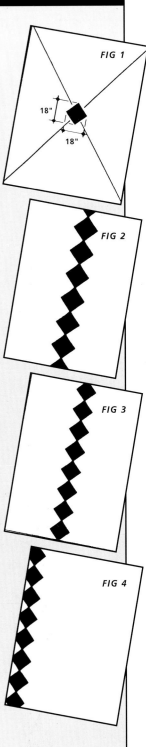

TEST YOUR COLOURS

4. Using test pots, paint a few squares of paper in your two chosen colours and lay them on the floor of the room you want to decorate. Leave them there for a day or two so that you can see how they look together and how light affects them. Varnish will affect the strength of the chosen colours too, so if possible test this as well.

5. Make sure that the surface of the floor is clean. The floor pictured on the previous page is painted on concrete but if you are decorating a wooden floor, it is a good idea to sand it down lightly beforehand.

6. With a roller or large paintbrush, seal the floor with the relevant primer. For wood, use a wood primer, for concrete use a sealer.

7. If you are using a dark/light colour scheme (eg black and white) you can speed things up by painting the light colour all over the floor now, before marking out the diamonds. It may need two coats for a good finish. With colours of equal strength, mark up the pattern on the primer base coat. Leave to dry.

ADDING ALTERNATE SQUARES

8. Find the centre of the floor by stretching two pieces of string at diagonals, – either from the corners of the room or the corners of your chosen rectangle. Pin the ends into the floor or skirting board. The centre of the room is where the string crosses. Using a pencil, mark this point.

STEP 8

STEP 9

STEP 9

STEP 10

STEP 10

9. Make a 30cm (12in) square template using the ruler and set square. Use this as a measuring guide and to double check your drawn squares. Measure halfway along one wall and lightly draw a line from this point to the centre. Using a set square, find the right angle and draw in the diagonal of your first diamond. Draw up the rest of your grid.

10. Use masking tape to outline alternate squares (see picture) ready for painting the first colour. (If you want a hand-painted look, paint squares free-hand using an artist's brush to paint edges.) Paint the squares with a 4cm (1 1/2in) brush, allow to dry and repeat the whole process with remaining squares of the first colour. Repeat using contrast colour until the floor is covered. Touch up any drip marks.

VARNISH

11. When thoroughly dry, clean and apply varnish. The more coats of varnish you use, the better as it will inevitably wear down with use. At least two are recommended, but you must be prepared to keep the area unused and clean while drying. If bits of fluff or hair get stuck to it between coats, the effect is ruined. If you want the floor to stay as fresh as the day it was painted, apply extra coats, especially in areas where wear and tear will be most obvious, ie by the sink in the kitchen or down the middle of a hall. If you want an aged look, wait after applying the first coat of varnish until it looks suitably 'distressed', then add two or three more.

Limed Effect Floorboards

Limed wood has an elegant white-washed appearance which subtly emphasizes the grain. It lends a cool Scandinavian feel to rooms and is widely used in kitchen and bedroom furniture. Floorboards, too, can be given a limed treatment.

you will need

- White gloss paint (the type that only requires a single coat is best)
- White spirit
- Sponge
- Paint brush
- Varnish

step by step
LIMED EFFECT FLOORBOARDS

1. Make sure the floorboards are clean and dust-free. Prime them with two coats of varnish thinned with white spirit. Leave the first coat to dry thoroughly before applying the second.

2. Mix the gloss paint with white spirit in equal proportions and paint on to the boards, a small area at a time.

3. Before the gloss dries, quickly wipe off the paint with a dry sponge.

4. The paint will soak into the grain of the wood while the surface has only a thin sponged wash, which gives an uneven, limed appearance.

5. To help protect the floor, coat with a heavy-duty varnish.

The plainest kitchen cupboards can be given a new lease of life with a coat of paint and a simple stencilled border. Experiment with different stencil designs before making your final decision.

Painted Melamine Kitchen Cupboards

Kitchens are notoriously expensive to replace from scratch. If you are stuck with old melamine units which you can't afford to replace, paint can help to give them an instant face-lift. This simple step by step guide will help you transform even the tattiest units and the end result looks so good that you won't think of it just as a temporary stopgap.

To give the kitchen a totally co-ordinated look, you could use an image from a patterned tile or kitchen curtains as the basis for your stencil. Or using a simple stencil, you could create a rectangular panel on each door, the centre of which may be filled with another decorative image.

you will need

- 'Wet and dry' abrasive paper
- Lint-free cloth
- Methylated spirit
- Zinc phosphate primer
- Gloss paint
- Paint brush
- Stencil
- Masking tape
- Eggshell paint

step by step
PAINTED MELAMINE CUPBOARDS

1. *To make the job easier, remove the doors. Scrub them twice with hot soapy water and fine grade 'wet and dry' abrasive paper to remove all dirt and grease. Leave the doors to dry thoroughly, then wipe over them with a soft lint-free cloth dampened with methylated spirit which will dry their surface immediately.*

2. *Paint on a base coat using zinc phosphate primer. When completely dry, paint a top coat of gloss paint, ensuring that it is smooth and evenly spread, and allow to dry thoroughly.*

3. *Using masking tape, fix the stencil you have chosen to the edge of the door and using eggshell paint, carefully dab on each colour making sure that you don't overload the brush. It is a good idea to practise this technique and the combination of colours on a piece of card or off-cut of wood.*

4. *When you have added all the colours, wait until they dry thoroughly before carefully removing the stencil.*

Painted tiles

Using gloss paint and good quality paint brushes to ensure a neat finish, you can paint a tromp l'oeil tiled wall in your bathroom or kitchen. Although you could use the same colour of paint throughout, it looks more effective when two or three shades are combined.

you will need

- White gloss paint
- Paint brush
- Pencil
- Masking tape
- Gloss paint in a second colour

step by step
PAINTED TILES

1. Make sure that the surface is clean and dust-free before applying two coats of white glass paint with a 5 or 7.5cm (2 or 3in) brush.

2. When the surface is quite dry, mark a square grid on to the wall with pencil. You can decide what size you'd like the tiles – here they are around 15cm (6 in) square.

3. Decide on the squares that you want to paint the same colour and carefully line the sides of each one with masking tape. Paint each square with a 2.5cm (1in) brush.

4. When the first colour has dried, repeat the process for the second colour of gloss paint and continue until the wall is covered. Remember to leave a slight gap between the 'tiles' for 'grouting'. Top the tiles off with a striking triangular border, painted in the same way.

This painted trompe l'oeil tiled splashback is hard to tell from the real thing and it's remarkably quick and easy to do.

CHAPTER THREE

Paper

Wallpaper offers a wonderful range of decorative possibilities. It can provide a restrained background against which you can display pictures and prints or can be a feature in itself. Whatever the style of your home, there is bound to be a suitable wallpaper.

Where to start

The choice of wallpapers and borders is quite simply staggering and you could be forgiven for feeling swamped by the variety of different designs. And not only is there a choice of patterns but also a choice of stockists – everywhere from up-market interior design showrooms to the huge DIY 'sheds' now sell wallpaper and borders.

So if, understandably, you feel confused, the simplest place to start is with a specialist showroom or department within a shop. Most of them display new wallpaper and border collections in co-ordinated pages of vast books. These books not only provide an ideal way of viewing designs at close range, but give as accurate an idea as possible of how the co-ordinates will work once in situ. Obviously there are no rules that dictate you must stick with the manufacturer's suggested combinations, but the way pattern books are put together will help you to come up with ideas for decorating and help you to gain confidence. And once you feel more at ease with the sheer number of collections available, you can begin to mix designs from different sources to create a look that is unique to you. Some suppliers may be able to provide sample pieces of paper and borders for you to take home to check the patterns go with existing furnishings.

Making a choice

As well as the vast choice of patterns and designs around, wallpaper itself comes in different forms and finishes.

Lining Paper
Used as an absorbent surface to paint or to cover with decorative paper. Follow manufacturer's advice on whether lining walls is necessary,

Woodchip
Small pieces of wood give the paper a textured finish which makes it ideal for disguising poor surfaces. This paper should be painted when it has been hung.

Vinyl
As it is coated with plastic, vinyl papers are very robust and may be scrubbed clean. Ideal for kitchens and bathrooms.

Spongeable Papers
Though they may be wiped with a damp cloth, these papers are not suitable for heavy wear and tear.

PAINT EFFECT PAPERS
Perhaps it is not surprising, with the current interest in paint effects such as marbling and stippling, that papers which mimic different painted surfaces are so popular. If you feel inspired by the subtle nuances of colour and shade which are the hallmark of many paint effects, yet feel that you have neither the time nor the inclination to try them out at home, paint effect wallpaper could provide the answer. These papers are amongst the most versatile of all wallpaper. Not only do

LEFT *You don't have to confine border paper to cornices and dado rails. Offcuts may be used to decorate simple wooden shelves.*

they range from boldly-patterned marble to subtly sponged and stippled designs, but they are also generally available in a wide range of colours. While the colour range will be more restricted than when working with paint, papers undoubtedly offer a more straightforward means of decorating. However, you can be just as creative with wallpaper as any other material.

Paint effect papers are ideal for combining with other papers, paint finishes and borders. Make a sample board of various colours and textures before making your final decision, and then make a drawing of the wall or room that you intend to decorate. Stick small samples of paper in place in the drawing to get some idea of the finished result.

MARBLED PAPERS

If you want to create an air of instant opulence, marbled wallpaper is ideal. The paper comes in two types – designs which are based on man-made marbling of the sort that is used on the inside covers of old books and, more commonly, patterns inspired by natural quarried marble. The first type of paper has a dense pattern and may involve several different colours.

With wallpaper designed to look like slabs of natural marble, you can either opt for soft shades of cream, grey, pink or ochre which echo the colours of the real thing or choose more dramatic colours like dark red and emerald green to create a surreal fantasy in jewel-like shades. Whatever you decide on, marble papers of all colours are ideal for cutting into the shape of pillars, columns, balustrades and panels so that you can create trompe l'oeil effects. It can also be used in conjunction with architecturally inspired paper borders to create a classical style room.

DRAGGED PAPERS

Dragging is one of the most elegant effects and there are many wallpapers which are based on this understated stripe. Dragged

papers have a slightly formal air and are often used in halls and dining rooms. They provide a subtle means of accentuating height and work well with patterns or a more defined stripe.

When choosing a dragged paper, you should be aware that the stripe tends to look more obvious in darker colours: in lighter shades the effect will barely show. Try to borrow large samples of paper to get a clear idea of how it will look once in place. And a final word of warning, be careful to follow hanging instructions precisely so that you don't end up with dark 'shadows' where the paper joins.

SPONGED PAPERS

Available in a wide range of colours, sponged wallpaper is amongst the most popular of designs. It's an ideal choice if you want to hang paintings and is versatile enough to be used in any room. Sponged papers provided a subtle background for print rooms too.

TROMPE L'OEIL

Wallpaper is an ideal accomplice if you want to master the fine art of deception. Trompe l'oeil papers come in many guises ranging from the simple paint effects mentioned above to detailed prints which can look like anything from swagged drapery to panelled bookcases.

Trompe l'oeil papers are a perfect way of introducing an element of fun and fantasy and often work well in small spaces where the effect is quite unexpected. You might like to try papering a small hallway in 'stone' to give the impression of a Medieval castle or decorating a bedroom with paper based on luxurious swags of fabric. Rather than go to the trouble of having expensive features like marble panelling or a hand-painted mural incorporated in your home, it is often cheaper and simpler to fake them with wallpaper. And as the end result isn't a permanent fixture, you'll easily be able to change the paper when you get tired of it.

BELOW *Reinstate the style of bygone days with textured dado panels. This design, reminiscent of Art Nouveau, has been painted a soft grey to tone with the curtains.*

RIGHT *The popularity of Arts and Crafts wallpapers never seems to diminish. Designers of the original patterns drew on natural themes such as leaves, birds and flowers for inspiration.*

TEXTURED AND EMBOSSED PAPERS

If your walls are uneven or beginning to crack, textured papers can hide a multitude of sins. The main benefit of these papers is that they help to disguise flawed surfaces and provide an interesting surface which can be painted to co-ordinate with your colour scheme. And these days, with the great range of patterns available, there's no need to stick with woodchip. Textured and embossed papers come in everything from random abstracts, which are well-suited to modern schemes, to classically-inspired designs and Victorian-style repeat patterns.

As well as standard wallpaper, you can also buy textured panels which can be used to create dados or panelled walls: this is especially useful in modern houses with little architectural interest. Borders, too, are available in relief patterns. Often based on traditional designs, they can be stuck to the contours of a plain, modern cornice to give the impression of original plasterwork and so make it look more interesting.

ARTS AND CRAFTS

Based on natural forms such as flowers and leaves and designed over a hundred years ago, these papers remain popular today and many original designs continue to be printed. Common elements of these designs include foliage, birds and berries which are worked into distinct, two-dimensional patterns. Although there is a pattern repeat, it is not always evident which distinguishes them from single motif repeat patterns.

Authentic Arts and Crafts papers were often used in beamed and panelled rooms but they will look good in virtually any setting – especially the relatively intimate proportions of terraced houses or cottages where the organic quality and sophisticated shades of colour can be appreciated.

STRIPED PAPERS

Striped papers have a timeless quality which makes them a popular choice for both traditional and modern homes. The range of available colours is excellent and the variety of different widths of stripe makes these papers particularly versatile. In some papers, the stripes vary very subtly in shade, giving an elegant shadowy appearance while others make use of contrasting colours, often with dramatic results.

Whichever look you prefer, striped paper will give an illusion of added height so is useful for rooms with low ceilings or areas where you'd like to create an impression of space. Although it tends to look quite formal, striped papers in brighter shades can be used to create a beach-hut feel.

Hanging Wallpaper

Preparation

- Remove old wallcoverings by soaking them with a solution of warm water and washing-up liquid, or use a stripping agent. Scrape the paper away with a stripping knife.
- For woodchip, embossed or washable papers, hire a wallpaper stripper from a DIY centre or local hire shop.
- Vinyl wall coverings have a paper backing which is left behind when you peel off the top surface. This should be soaked and removed as above, or if it is in good condition it may be used as a base.
- Walls must be clean, sound and dry before you start work. Fill cracks and holes with filler and smooth with sandpaper when dry.
- Recently plastered walls need to be 'sized' with solution of diluted paste to seal them.
- Always check the instructions on your paper for advice on whether lining paper is required. If in doubt, ask your retailer.

Before you start

- Check that the rolls are from the same batch.
- Ensure that the pattern is the correct way.
- Check the order of hanging.
- Always mark a vertical line on each wall before you start hanging. Use a plumb line or long spirit level to mark the vertical each time you turn a corner.
- If you are papering a ceiling as well as walls, do the ceiling first.

Cutting

- Measure the height of the wall and cut a corresponding length of paper, allowing an extra 5cm (2in) top and bottom for trimming.
- With boldly patterned papers, cut the length so that after trimming, there will be a complete motif at the top.
- Use your first cut length as a guide for further pieces – match patterns carefully.
- Mark a scale along the edge of your pasting table to help with measuring.
- Re-check length before cutting. Use a sharp trimming knife and straight edge.
- Remember to mark any existing screw holes (from shelves for example) as soon as you have hung the paper, while you can still see where they are. Mark with matchsticks so you can locate them when the paper has dried.

1. *Mix paste according to instructions on the packet. Place the first cut length face-down on the pasting table. With a pasting brush, brush the paste along the entire length and work it out towards the edges. Try to ensure that the paper overlaps the table slightly to prevent paste getting on the patterned side of the paper.*

2. *Leave the pasted paper for a few minutes to absorb enough moisture for it to become supple. This also helps to avoid wrinkles and bubbles when the paper is hung. The time you need to leave it will depend on the type of paper – read instructions on the label. Fold pasted surfaces together, bringing top and bottom to meet in the middle. For longer lengths, fold like a concertina.*

3. *Check which is the top end of the length and carry the folded paper over one arm to the wall.*

4. *Hold the top corners, open the top fold and stick the top half of the length on the wall. Then, allowing 5cm (2in) at the ceiling line for trimming, slide the paper exactly into position. Smooth down the middle of the paper with the paper-hanging brush, working out towards the edges to remove the wrinkles and air bubbles as you go.*

HANGING WALLPAPER

5. *Unfold the rest of the paper and continue to smooth down, leaving a similar trimming margin of 5cm (2in) at the bottom of the wall.*

6. *Run the back of your scissors along the angle of the ceiling and skirting to mark where the paper has to be trimmed. Gently pull the paper away from the wall and trim off excess. Wipe off excess paste from the ceiling and skirting with a damp sponge, and brush down the edges of the paper.*

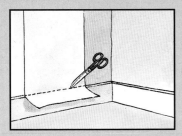

7. *Position the next length of paper on the wall beside the first and slide it into position so that the pattern matches at eye level. Wrinkles appear if there are still air pockets under the paper. Gently peel back the paper and brush it down again. Minor wrinkles should disappear on drying.*

8. *If necessary, gently use a seam roller to flatten joins about 20 minutes after hanging. Don't roll embossed or relief papers.*

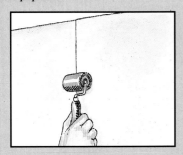

9. *Never hang a full width of paper around a corner; always hang the paper in two parts. First measure the distance from the last piece you have hung to the*

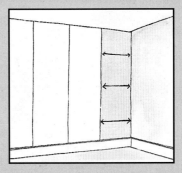

corner. Do this at several points from skirting to ceiling to find the greatest distance.

10. *Cut a strip of paper 1cm (1/2in) wider than this distance, paste and hang it with the extra paper overlapping onto the next wall. Measure the width of the off-cut from the corner and mark a vertical this distance from the corner on to the side wall. Paste the off-cut, aligning the uncut edge with the vertical line so that the cut edge fits flush into the corner and covers the overlap. Treat external corners in the same way.*

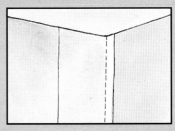

11. *Before papering around a light switch or socket, turn off electricity at the mains – don't forget you are using water. Smooth the length of paper very gently over the fitting. For square fittings, pierce the paper at the centre of the fitting and make four diagonal cuts from the centre to approximately 2.5cm (1in) beyond each corner.*

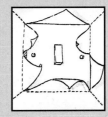

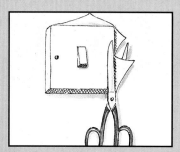

paper while you work. The basic method is the same as for papering a wall, but remember to paper the ceiling before the walls. Paper across the room, working away from the window. Before you start, mark a straight guideline on the ceiling about 1cm (1/2in) less than one paper width away from the wall.

12. *Press the paper round the edge of the fitting and lightly pencil round the outline. Trim away the excess, leaving 3-4mm (1/8-1/6in) extra all around to brush behind the plate. Partially unscrew the plate and pull it away from the wall. Brush the paper behind the plate and screw back in place. Never brush metallic or foil wall coverings behind the plate as they could conduct electricity. Instead, cut to fit around the switch.*

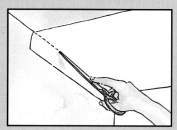

15. *Cut a length of paper, allowing 5cm (2in) overlap at each end. Paste and fold the paper as before. Position paper against the guideline, supporting the folds with a roll of paper or similar object. Unfold little by little and brush into position. Score and trim each end.*

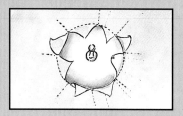

13. *For round switches, make a series of star-shaped cuts in the paper, press down, mark and trim in the same way.*

14. *Papering a ceiling can be difficult for a beginner working alone. It is better to have a helper to support lengths of*

MEASURING UP

Use this chart to work out how many rolls of wallpaper you will need. Figures are based on a standard roll of around 10.05m/11 yards in length and 53cm/2ft 1in wide. Remember that for larger patterns you will need more rolls to allow for matching the design.

WALL HEIGHT FROM SKIRTING	THE COMPLETE DISTANCE AROUND THE ROOM INCLUDING WINDOWS AND DOORS												
	9m (30ft)	10m (34ft)	12m (38ft)	14m (46ft)	16m (54ft)	18m (62ft)	21m (70ft)	22m (74ft)	23m (78ft)	24m (82ft)	26m (86ft)	28m (94ft)	30m (98ft)
2.15 – 2.3m (7ft – 7ft 6in)	4	5	5	6	7	8	9	10	10	11	12	13	13
2.3 – 2.45m (7ft 6in – 8ft)	5	5	6	7	8	9	10	10	11	11	12	13	14
2.45 – 2.6m (8ft – 8ft 6in)	5	5	6	7	9	10	11	12	12	13	14	15	15
2.6 – 2.75m (8ft 6in – 9ft)	5	5	6	7	9	10	11	12	12	13	14	15	15
2.75 – 2.9m (9ft – 9ft 6in)	6	6	7	8	9	10	12	12	13	14	14	15	16
2.9 – 3.05m (9ft 6in – 10ft)	6	6	7	8	10	11	12	13	14	14	15	16	17
3.05 – 3.2m (10ft – 10ft 6in)	6	7	8	9	10	12	13	14	15	16	16	18	19

PAPERING AN ARCHWAY

To paper an archway, paper the facing wall first, allowing an extra 2.5cm (1in) of paper around the inside of the arch. Cut V-shaped pieces out of this hem so that you are left with a saw-tooth effect. Turn in the teeth so that they lie flat on the inside of the arch and cut two pieces of paper, one to run up each side to meet in the centre at the top.

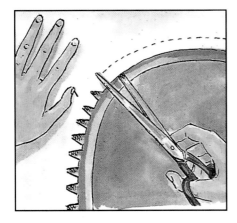

Wallpaper Borders

Whether your taste is for sophisticated rooms wallpapered from skirting to ceiling, or you prefer the simplicity of painted surfaces, border papers are an invaluable way of adding interest and vitality. They provide a quick and easy means of changing the appearance of a room and come in every type of design from traditional florals to friezes inspired by ancient architecture.

Not only are they generally inexpensive, but wallpaper borders are extremely versatile with applications far beyond the tried and tested cornice line. And you don't have to be an expert to put some interesting ideas for border papers into action.

HANGING BORDERS

Draw a pencil line on the wall as a guide and cut a piece of border the full length of the wall. Paste the border and fold it concertina fashion. Then, using a line as a guide, unfold the border and brush it into place. Corners around a door or window should be mitred: overlap borders where

they meet and draw a diagonal line across the corner. Cut along the line through both layers, using a craft knife. Remove excess pieces.

THE PRACTICALITIES

While designs and patterns are largely a matter of personal choice, the dimensions of a room influence the depth of the border you choose. A narrow border, a couple of inches wide, is going to have little effect in a large room while one of the deeper, more opulent designs is liable to dominate a tiny room. If you are finding it difficult to visualise which width is best, try to get large sample lengths of border and stick them in placed with Blu-tack to give you a better idea of the finished result.

Of course, even within one collection border papers come in a variety of depths. This gives you tremendous scope to combine several borders within one room where different depths are suited to different purposes.

EXISTING FEATURES

Many very modern homes have little, if any, architectural detail. A great number of wallpaper borders, based on classical motifs, such as egg and dart, acanthus leaves and fluting, provide an ideal way of adding instant architecture. Starting with the barest shell, you can add features such as cornicing, dado and even panelling – all with paper and paste. On the other hand, if your home has existing cornicing, you should be careful that whatever you choose does not detract from it.

Panels

One of the most useful decorating devices around, panels are relatively quick and easy to make using cut lengths of wallpaper border. These large scale rectangles may be 'filled' with contrasting paper or may simply provide a framework within which to display pictures, for example. However you choose to use wallpaper panels, you will find that it helps to plan the arrangement on a piece of squared paper before you start cutting and pasting. Experiment with borders of different widths and styles too. Once you become adept, you may be able to come up with arrangements that incorporate more than one border paper.

Relatively small scale panels may be used to create a focal point on a wall, for example above a fireplace, and provide a setting for framed pictures or mirrors. Larger panels are ideal for breaking space down into more manageable proportions. You could create a panel-effect dado or transform a long narrow corridor simply by applying borders cleverly. With practice you might like to attempt more dramatic effects by combining paint effect papers in two different shades or styles (sponged and marbled papers work well together).

Panelled Doors

If you prefer the appearance of traditional panelled doors but are stuck with plain wooden ones, a quick way of transforming them is to use border papers to create instant panelling. Don't try to recreate a complex multi-panelled door but stick to one or two large panels. You could fill the panel and the surrounding area with contrasting papers or use large scale images (cut from rolls of wallpaper) within each of the frames.

OTHER IDEAS FOR USING BORDER PAPER

Once you start to think of wallpaper border not merely as a last-minute detail but a decorative device in its own right, you'll find

that there are boundless opportunities for using it imaginatively.

- Use borders to frame windows and doors. This is especially useful at small windows where conventional window treatments would not be feasible.
- Make a feature of shelves or other display areas by sticking lengths of border to the wall behind them.
- Wallpaper may be cut into a pointed or scalloped 'pelmet' to create an effective alternative to conventional border paper.
- Use a template to keep the design accurate and, if you are using a patterned paper, make sure that it is a design that works as well sideways as vertically.
- Use panels of wallpaper border to add interest to plain doors or even cupboard

LEFT *Plain walls can be broken up into more interesting proportions with panels made from lengths of wallpaper border.*

BELOW *A pretty as well as practical application for a wallpaper border, this small cottage window has been framed with a lilac-patterned design which not only accentuates the window but also allows in as much light as possible.*

ABOVE *Although it looks as if it has been carefully hand-stencilled, this elegant border is actually printed on a clear background so that it can be used against any background colour.*

RIGHT *Print rooms look stunning and the joy is that no two are alike. The linking bows, rosettes and ribbons are quite intricate, so allow yourself plenty of time to cut them out!*

doors. Seal them with a coat of clear matt varnish to help keep the paper in good condition.

PRINT ROOMS

Create your own modern day print room with coloured borders stuck in frames around prints. Use anything from wrapping paper, old calendars and catalogues for reference material.

Popular in the eighteenth century, print rooms offered the opportunity for amateur collectors to show off their prints in a captivatingly original way. The prints, which cost relatively little, were arranged in groups and pasted directly on to the wall. They were framed and linked with specially printed borders and motifs (such as ribbons and rosettes) and the combination of intricate design and monochrome colouring looked stunning whether against subtle cream walls or more dramatically coloured backgrounds.

Today it is still possible to buy paper sheets of decorative details used in the past to make print rooms. There's no need to worry if you don't have a collection of original prints ready to hang: there are contemporary alternatives that will work just as well. Scour junk shops and jumble sales for old catalogues, illustrated books and prints. If you don't want to use original

reference material, it's easy to photocopy the images you like. If the photocopy looks too new, sponge a solution of tea over it to give the illusion of age.

It's best to start with a small area (bathrooms and hallways are ideal). Gather together the main images and make a rough sketch of how you want them to appear on the wall. Start your design off with the largest prints and then add the smaller ones. With a sharp craft knife, cut out sufficient border for framing the prints (if you are working with monotones, you'll find it easy to mix several different styles on one wall) as well as a selection of decorative motifs that will link the various images. The designs are quite intricate so will take time to cut out. Mark all these elements on your sketch so that you are sure that you have a fairly clear idea of how the finished print room will look.

Take time positioning the pictures on the wall. If necessary, Blu-tack them in place so that you can rearrange them until you are completely satisfied. Stick the images in place with conventional wallpaper paste (you may find it easier to work with a weaker solution than normal). Add the 'frames' and finally the motifs until the entire wall is covered. For extra protection, coat the images with acrylic varnish.

Designer Tips for Print Rooms

- Make sure that you have enough images, border and decorative motifs cut before you start work.
- For a well-balanced design, there should be a good number of prints or pictures so that the decorated wall is well covered.
- You don't have to stick to rectangles and squares. Some prints lend themselves to oval, circular or even octagonal shapes. The print room papers already mentioned have special borders to complement these shapes.
- If you feel unsure about where to start, choose a small area and make it a simple arrangement of two or four 'frames'.

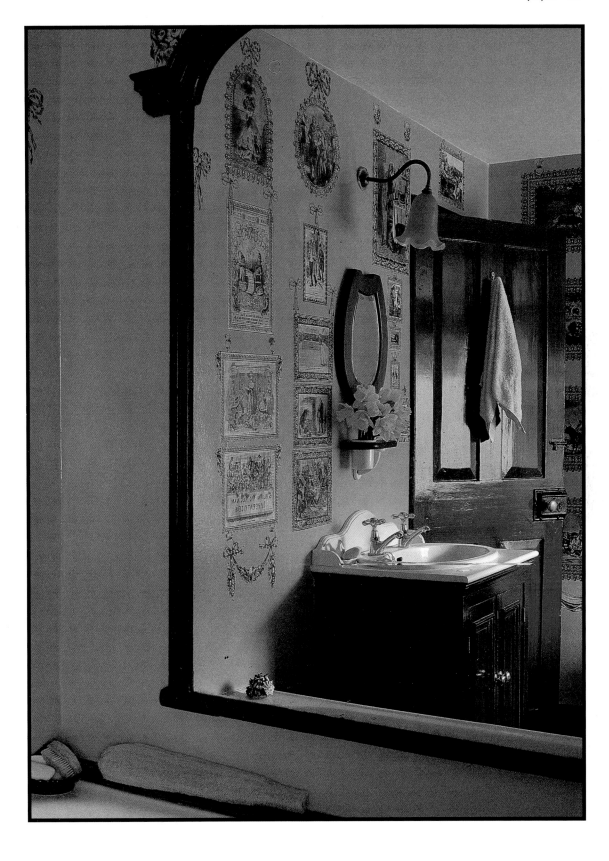

Once you start looking, you'll find sources for découpage in everything from wrapping paper to wallpaper border. You can even buy special découpage sourcebooks full of black and white and colour images.

- The background must be fairly plain. You may use paint or wallpaper, but don't choose anything more obtrusive than a sponged or dragged effect.
- Use images of various scales to add interest to your print room arrangement.
- Try to stick to some sort of theme, such as botanical or architectural prints. Or you might like to try making a room using images from local history, such as buildings, landmarks and famous characters.
- Use a spirit level and ruler to ensure that the main images are hung evenly.
- You can decorate plain doors and screens with small scale versions of print rooms.

Découpage

Another method of covering screens and other small accessories is découpage. Using decorative images cut out from wrapping paper, for example, you can arrange them to form a coherent picture. Although time-consuming (layers and layers of varnish must be applied to protect the paper and disguise the cut edges), découpage is fun to do and very rewarding. It is probably easiest to start with small items, before you work your way up to tackling something like a screen.

Like print rooms, you can use a variety of sources. You could incorporate images that have sentimental value, such as photographs, and for an updated version of découpage, you might like to use pictures cut from souvenirs such as tickets, Christmas cards, postcards or theatre programmes. Quicker and easier still, découpage looks very effective when made from brightly-coloured scraps. Much-loved by the Victorians, specially printed sheets of scraps may be bought today and as they are ready-cut, provide an instant means of decoration. Small personalised items, like boxes, also make special gifts for friends and family.

CHAPTER FOUR

FABRIC

From opulent velvet and brocade to humble gingham and muslin, fabrics come in every weight, colour and design imaginable. Even for those who are familiar with the wonderful array of materials on the market, the sheer choice can be baffling. However, it is the very range of different cloths which makes this such an exciting medium. Don't worry if you have never sewn a stitch in your life – there are shortcuts that the most inexperienced homemaker can take.

What To Look For When Choosing Fabric

No matter what project you have in mind, there are certain points that you should consider when you are looking for material. It is important that the fabric you buy is suitable for the job for which it is intended: upholstery must be able to withstand a lot of wear and tear, sheets must be washable and sheer curtains must let in light while maintaining your privacy.

CONTENT

The actual fibres that make up any fabric affect it in a number of ways including its appearance, how it drapes and whether it is easy to wash and iron. These days there is a tendency to opt for natural fibres such as cotton and wool, but many soft furnishing fabrics are made up from a mixture of natural and synthetic fibres. The synthetic is usually there for a good reason, normally making a fabric easier to handle or to prevent it from crushing (a good example of such a combination is polycotton sheeting). Neither natural or synthetic fabric is better but one may be more suitable for a particular job than the other.

WIDTH

Most furnishing fabric comes in widths of 137 or 150cm (54 or 60in), but these figures do vary so always check before you buy. Imported fabrics in particular are likely to differ from the norm, and there are even designs which appear to be standard width but which, in fact, are doubled over on the roll. Other fabrics such as ticking, wadding and interlining follow their own rules.

SHRINKAGE

While most manufacturers will advise dry cleaning as opposed to washing even plain cotton, you will probably be tempted to throw unlined curtains, cushion covers and loose covers in the washing machine. This is something of a risk, but to avoid disasters test a sample piece of fabric beforehand to check for colour fastness, shrinkage etc.

PATTERN REPEAT

The pattern on a fabric, be it printed or woven, should be taken into consideration when you are estimating quantities. The repeat is the distance measured vertically from the start of the pattern to the point where the pattern next appears. For curtains using more than a width of fabric for each drape, the pattern where two widths join must match – and the inner edge of each drape should also match so that when the curtains are pulled, the gap is unobtrusive.

Obviously the larger the pattern repeat, the more potential waste there will be. Many traditional chintzes feature bold floral designs originally designed with large scale windows and rooms in mind. Although these same fabrics can look stunning in

Simple Roman blinds are a practical choice for kitchens. These brightly striped blinds accentuate the elegant proportions of the unusual windows.

modern homes too, you should only use them where you can feel confident that they are not going to dominate a small area. Smaller prints are less wasteful and it is easy to make use of any scraps, too. Stripes, while they do not have a vertical pattern repeat to consider, should be matched across the fabric so that joins do not show.

The broader the stripe, the more obvious any mismatch, so take care when running up seams.

There is advice on page 69 on estimating curtain fabric and how to allow for pattern repeats. It is always advisable, however, to double check with the shop you are buying from before ordering.

DISCONTINUED RANGES

Always check whether the range you have chosen is likely to be discontinued in the near future. Although the lifespan of any range is hard to define, if it continues to sell well, the manufacturer will generally continue to produce it. As new designs are launched, however, so old ones must be withdrawn to make room for them. Bear this in mind if your long term plans involve buying extra lengths of co-ordinating fabric.

Keep a fabric swatch with details of.reference number and description of colour. If possible, take a note of the manu-facturing company's address so if you have difficulty in finding the fabric in future, you can contact them direct for a list of stockists.

Types of fabric

Brocade

May be self-coloured or multi-coloured. A slight three-dimensional (raised) pattern that is normally floral, brocade may be woven from a number of materials including viscose, cotton and polyester. It comes in different weights which may be used for anything from upholstery to curtaining.

Broderie anglais

Plain-weave cotton featuring a distinctive punched hole pattern. The holes may be circular or shaped and are normally finished in white cotton, though coloured thread is sometimes used. Lengths of broderie anglais are often used instead of traditional lace.

Buckram

A very stiff material which is made from cotton coated in size to make it tough. Buckram may be used to stiffen pelmets or curtain tie-backs but is only appropriate for more formal window treatments.

Canvas

Made from heavyweight unbleached cotton or linen, canvas is used for deckchairs, windbreaks, hammocks and other outdoor furniture. Open-weave canvas provides the base for a lot of embroidery.

Chenille

A fabric which has a distinctive pile similar to heavy velvet, chenille is available either plain or patterned. In patterned varieties the soft pile is combined with a plain woven background to create a contrast of textures. Popular in Victorian times, chenille is enjoying something of a revival. It may be used for tablecloths and curtains, although these days it is most widely used as upholstery fabric.

Chintz (Glazed chintz)

A cotton fabric which is associated with traditional floral prints, chintz is finely woven and has a special finish which helps to make it resistant to dirt. Glazed chintz has a different finish which gives the fabric a high sheen, making it ideal for curtains and other soft furnishings. Allow for shrinkage – and beware that after a number of cleanings, the sheen may begin to dull.

Cotton satin

A popular choice for curtains, cotton satin is the product of specially woven cotton with a sheen on one side. It normally comes in plain colours.

Crewelwork

Increasingly popular, crewelwork is usually imported from India and is often wool, but sometimes cotton-, based. A heavy fabric with distinctive embroidered designs, crewelwork is available either self-coloured or with coloured wools on a cream (or occasionally black) background.

Damask

A traditional fabric which was originally woven in silk, these days damask may be woven in any number of materials. Widely used for curtains, table linen and upholstery, damask is usually self-coloured but may be two-toned (shot effect).

Flannelette

Associated with sheets and nightclothes, flannelette has a soft, peach-skin feel and comes in plain colours (usually pastels) and stripes.

Gingham

A checked cotton fabric which is made up of one colour and white, gingham is enjoying a revival and has encouraged the manufacture of a wide variety of checked fabrics. Reminiscent of Shaker or American country-style.

Hessian

Like gingham, hessian is once again very popular. Normally woven from jute, hessian is available in different weights and finishes from coarse sacking to fine cloth suitable for curtains. Hessian is an inexpensive way of adding textural interest to a room.

Here a simple blind framed by dress curtains provides the ideal opportunity for mixing patterns. The curtains have a narrow gingham trim to tie in with the fabric of the blind.

Linen

Made from flax, linen is often mixed with other fibres such as cotton and wool. Very robust, linen may be printed to co-ordinate with anything from floral chintzes to kelim patterns. There is a growing trend to use linen in its natural form.

Moire

Traditionally woven in silk, moire is more often a synthetic fabric these days. Its trademark water pattern has a classic appeal and may also be used in wallpaper.

Muslin or butter muslin

A very lightweight sheer cotton fabric which is very cheap. Muslin's soft texture makes it ideal for draping and it is becoming a popular substitute for conventional net curtains. It has a tendency to shrink so consider that when you are working out quantities. Used also for bed drapes and 'mosquito net' hangings.

Paisley

Originally from Scotland though the scrolled patterns themselves derive from India, paisley cloth was originally woven in wool although these days paisley patterns are woven or printed on to a wide range of cloth.

PVC

Generally a cotton fabric with a plastic-type finish which makes it waterproof, PVC is widely used for tablecloths, and is especially useful for outdoor use, eg tablecloths for garden furniture.

Sheeting

Available in a wide range of colours, patterned and plain, sheeting is wider than most fabrics (228cm/90in) so is ideal for making duvet covers, sheets and pillow-cases. Sheeting is generally made from a poly cotton mix, making it easy to care for. Its width makes it useful in other areas too, eg lightweight bedroom curtains.

Ticking

A closely woven fabric which is normally striped, ticking is used for pillows and mattresses as it is featherproof. Now gaining in popularity in other areas of home furnishing, eg curtains.

Fabric for Windows

Windows are amongst your home's most important features. Both internally and on the exterior they help to give your home its particular character. The variety of architectural styles, ranging from modern picture windows often seen in bungalows and blocks of flats to bay windows and elegant sash and case designs associated with older properties, is enormous.

While the number of window styles is great, the options for dressing them is greater still. From ready-made curtains and blinds to opulently swagged and beribboned custom-made designs, the choice is staggering. The most luxurious and expensive window treatments are by no means always the most appropriate, however, and the trick of successful window dressing is to find a style that is suitable for not only the type of window but the character of the interior. There's no point in choosing stark Roman blinds for a cosy, cottage living room and luxuriously draped curtains will look out of place in a kitchen where practicality is a major concern.

TYPES OF TREATMENTS

The way that you dress your windows will influence the overall appearance of a room. Curtains or blinds can set the tone of a room and may even dictate the furnishings you choose. Although there are many variations on these basic themes, window dressings fall into the following varieties.

Roller blind

A simple blind that works on a roller mechanism. The fabric, which should match the size of the window or its surround exactly, is stiffened to give a crisp finish. The blind may be fitted inside or outside the window recess and is most often used in kitchens and bathrooms, though brightly patterned designs are popular in children's rooms, too. Kits and spray-on-fabric stiffener are available so you can make roller blinds in your own fabric. Whether you do this or buy the blinds ready-made, they are probably the least expensive of all window treatments as very little fabric is required.

Roman blind

A simple yet stylish blind which, like a roller blind, may be fitted either inside the window recess or mounted on the window surround. Roman blinds have a distinctive slatted appearance and fold into concertina-like pleats when drawn up. Their tailored appearance is well-suited to plain fabrics or those with an understated design, but if you want to dress them up, decorative fabric borders work well sewn round the outer

The most understated trim can transform a plain blind. These Roman blinds are given a stylish finish with a double border and a looped effect along the top.

edge. Also relatively inexpensive, Roman blinds are popular with people who prefer a no-frills approach to home decorating. They are relatively easy to make from kits but are rarely found ready-made.

Austrian blind

A luxurious frilled blind which has a ruched appearance when drawn up. When the blind is let down, however, the ruching eases out until only the bottom edge maintains its decorative gathers.

Venetian blind

A horizontally slated blind which, although once associated with office environments, now comes in a wide range of colours and finishes, making it useful in kitchens and bathrooms. The slats themselves are available in different widths for different effects.

Vertical slatted blind

Working on the same lines as a Venetian blind, a slatted blind with the slats hung vertically rather than horizontally.

Festoon blind

When drawn up, a festoon blind is indistinguishable from an Austrian blind. As it is made from fabric which measures twice the window drop, however, when pulled down it will continue to have a very ruched appearance from top to bottom.

Paper and cane blinds

Paper blinds, slatted with light wooden battens have a distinctly Oriental feel and, as they are semi-translucent, allow light to filter into the room while obscuring the view. Cane blinds, on the other hand, have an old colonial appeal. Like paper blinds, they are relatively inexpensive and as they are available ready to hang, provide an instant window-dressing solution.

Lace panels

Ready-made lace panels look wonderful against the light where their intricate

FAR LEFT *Anything more ornate than a pleated blind would detract from the opulence of this classically-inspired bathroom.*

LEFT *Lace is perfect for masking a less than picturesque view. Lace panels are particularly easy to hang and look good in modern or traditional settings.*

Café curtains not only maintain a degree of privacy but also allow you a glimpse of the outside world.

designs are easily seen. If you can't find the correct size for your window, furnishing lace can be sewn into a panel. To make life easy, you could use curtain clips to hang the panel.

Café curtains

Hanging from halfway down the window, these softly gathered curtains have a bright and informal appearance. Great for blocking out unsightly views, they are often used in bathrooms and kitchens. Cafe curtains are available in various depths. All you have to do is hem the edges and slot the curtain over a narrow pole or wire cord. The same idea can also be used to make a deeply

frilled pelmet which hangs from the top of the window.

Curtains

Ranging from opulently swagged and draped designs reminiscent of old theatre curtains to simply gathered sheer fabric, curtains come in every style imaginable. Though custom-made designs are certainly not cheap, you get exactly what you want. The choice of ready-made curtains, though more restricted, is improving all the time. Whichever you decide on, you'll find that curtains make a tremendous difference to your room.

HOW TO ESTIMATE FABRIC

1. Measure the width of the track or pole, not the width of the window. The track should ideally extend about 15cm (6in) either side of the window so that, when the curtains are drawn back, as much light as possible is allowed in. Multiply by two (for double width curtains or more if the tape requires it).

2. Divide this width by the width of the fabric and round the figure up unless only a fraction over (eg 2.05 could be rounded down to 2). The figure that you get is the number of widths of fabric required for your curtains.

3. Length: now measure from the track or pole to the floor (or however long you want the curtains to be). Add 30cm (12in) to allow for headings and hems.

4. Pattern repeat: ask if the size of the repeat is not clear. In this example, the repeat is 22cm (8 1/2in) and the drop is 2.3m (7 1/2ft) – make sure that you include the 30cm (12in) allowance in this calculation. Divide the total drop by the size of the repeat so, in this example, 230cm ÷ 22cm = 10.45 (7 1/2ft ÷ 8 1/2in = 10.45). Round this figure up to 11. You will need 11 pattern repeats for each drop so multiply 11 x 22cm = 2.42m (11 x 8 1/2in = 2.6yds). Now simply multiply that figure by the number of drops you intend to use to get the total quantity of fabric required.

- If you can't afford custom-made curtains, buy ready-made designs and decorate them with your own tie-backs, swagged pelmets or by sewing contrasting fabric-covered buttons or bows to the heading.
- Curtains that have been made a few inches too long for the window, though not very practical, can be bunched into sumptuous folds on the floor to add an opulent air to more formal rooms.
- Fringed or bobble trimming adds interest to plain ready-made curtains.
- Though expensive, curtains lined in a contrast fabric help to pull colour schemes together and have a luxurious weighty feel.
- Lengths of curtain weights can be sewn into the hems of lightweight curtains to help them hang better.

- At corner windows, a single curtain held to one side often works better than a conventional pair.
- Swathe the curtain pole in co-ordinating fabric for added luxury.

Headings

The same curtains can take on a completely different appearance depending on the heading tape that is used. The tape will also dictate the width of fabric required. Formal window treatments could use anything from triple pleat to goblet pleat tape while random gathers or pencil pleats would be more appropriate for everyday styles.

Easy Ideas for Windows

It is easy to fall into the trap of thinking that the more opulent a window dressing, the better. From swags and tails to heavily interlined drapes, there are so many possibilities that it can be difficult to know where to start – but the real trick is knowing when to stop. The simplest ideas are often the best: some of the accessories available in high street shops enable you to give windows a professional-looking finish and, with small inventive touches, you can come up with a window dressing that suits your own personal style.

A quick and easy idea for small windows is this unusual treatment. Each curtain is seamed at the top, leaving a 2.5cm (1in) border and a pocket for the wooden pole to slide through. The pole should fit snugly into the pocket so that the fabric ruches up to give a frilled effect above the pole. These curtains do not move on the pole; instead they are held open by small hooks attached halfway down the inside edge of each curtain, and the front of the curtains, just below the pole. These are simply unhooked to close the curtains.

Large and small windows can benefit from this ingenious idea. Rather than use conventional heading tape and hooks, these cream calico curtains have fabric loops

which the metal pole slots through. The pelmet has been filled with scrunched up paper to puff them out.

DRESS CURTAINS

To look at, dress curtains are indistinguishable from ordinary curtains but there is one important difference. Although unable to open and close, dress curtains are often used to 'frame' or embellish windows with plain blinds or sheer panels. One main benefit is that while they look exactly like conventional curtains, dress curtains require far less fabric so can be useful if you're on a limited budget. Another practical applicable is that they may be used in situations where conventional drapes are not feasible – at French windows, for example. They can be used very effectively with all styles of blinds to create an opulent layered effect.

- Use single widths of expensive fabric to make dress curtains and hang them in front of a self-coloured blind create an opulent layered effect.
- Add interest to a sheer window treatment by adding dress curtains.
- Extend the track by 30cm (12in) either side of a narrow window and hang dress curtains so that they don't obscure the

window and give the impression of extra width.

- Maintain the illusion by tying back the curtains with tassels or cord.

There is a special treatment designed specifically for dress curtains that makes hanging them an incredibly quick and easy job. Rather than use conventional tape and hooks (which are redundant as the curtain is not designed to open and close), the tape comes in two parts which grip one another firmly when put together. One length is sewn to the curtain and the other has an adhesive backing which is simple peeled off and stuck to the window surround. The two facing pieces of tape have tiny 'teeth' which grip one another firmly when pressed together. This makes it easy to hang dress curtain in awkwardly shaped spaces such as archways.

CURTAIN CLIPS

Curtain clips are a godsend for anyone without the time or inclination for sewing. They comprise a hoop which the pole slots through as normal and a sprung set of 'teeth' which grip the fabric. Ideal for lightweight fabrics such as muslin and voile, the clips make heading tape and hooks

LEFT *Nautical-style eyelets make an informal and unusual heading for curtains and blinds. You can buy eyelet punches in kits from good haberdashery departments.*

BELOW *Especially useful for hanging sheer and lightweight fabrics, curtain clips are invaluable if you want to transform your windows quickly.*

Swagholders are an ingenious device which enable you to create professional-looking rosettes of fabric at the top of windows.

redundant and so enable you to dress windows in a matter of minutes. You can use them as a stop gap (until you decide on a more permanent treatment) or in place of conventional curtains and blinds.

When you are trying to decide on fabric for window treatments, curtain clips provide an invaluable method of displaying sample lengths. And they can also be used to hang tapestries or decorative panels of fabric from short poles. In fact there is no end to their uses: wherever you want to make an instant transformation, whether with bed hangings or lace panels at a window, curtain clips will help you complete the project in no time at all. Try transforming a window for a festive occasion by clipping a length of sari fabric or other metallic sheer so that it shows behind the everyday drapes.

SWAG HOLDERS

These curled metal brackets make it easy for anyone to create opulent swagged pelmets. They are fixed at either end of a curtain track and hold draped lengths of fabric in place, helping to form a soft, informal pelmet. You can bunch the fabric into rosettes or just twist it around and tuck it into the swag holder to keep it in place.

As the process requires no sewing and only takes as a matter of a few minutes, it is easy to change the style or fabric of the pelmet. You can use swag holders with curtains or blinds to decorate any window.

Ideas For Swag Holders

- Use a swag of fabric over a plain blind to soften the appearance of the window.
- Give your bed an instant make-over. Fix three swag holders, one above and at one at either side of your bed, then drape fabric into a luxurious canopy.
- Transform an ordinary sofa or divan into a day bed. Push it back against the wall and use swag holders to create a sumptuous hanging.
- As it is important not to skimp on

quantities, buy soft fabrics like muslin which drape well and cost very little.
- If your curtains are a plain colour, swag a length of co-ordinating gingham from the holders and make matching tie-hacks for a co-ordinated look.
- At corner windows drape the fabric as normal but leave a long 'tail' on one side and a short one on the other.

UNUSUAL TIE-BACKS

Although you can buy all sorts of tie-backs off-the-shelf or go to the expense of having something custom-made to match your curtains, the choice is fairly limited. If you're after something that's a bit different, try looking beyond the soft furnishing department of your local store for everyday objects which, with a little imagination and ingenuity, can be quickly transformed into surprisingly stylish tie-backs.

- Twisted lengths of fake foliage such as ivy work well with plain fabric or with prints inspired by natural forms.
- Thick cotton rope looks great with ticking stripes and adds a nautical touch to windows. You could either use a single piece or plait or twist different colours together.
- A fun idea for a child's room is to sew a chain of tiny teddy bears or other small toys together to form a tie-back. Use characters or images from patterned wallpaper for inspiration.
- Fake flowers can be used to create a wide range of effects. Twist the wire stems into linked chains or sew the flower heads on to a cord or plain fabric tie-backs. You could even try matching flowers to the print on the fabric.
- A hunk of raffia tied in a messy bow looks best against natural fibres such as linen or hessian.
- Christmas tree garlands can be used at windows for special occasions during the festive period and, if you avoid glittery designs, all year-round too. Good florists often have interesting accessories and are well worth investigating.

Bright rugs and throws can help to disguise an old sofa and provide a cheaper alternative solution to re-upholstering.

Fabric as a Wallcovering

Fabric-covered walls make a change from wallpaper though they can be expensive. If you want to try fabric as an alternative to paper, it is best to use something relatively inexpensive, such as ticking or Indian cotton. Though perhaps not as luxurious as the silk damasks which were originally used, they will be easier to handle and more affordable too.

Although you can stick fabric directly to the wall, you will get a more professional finish by stretching it on to wooden battens. Horizontal battens need to be fixed above the skirting board and at the finished height (usually the cornice or picture rail. Vertical battens should then be screwed slightly less than one fabric width apart using counter-sunk screws. Use battens for framing anything from doors to light switches so that you can fit the fabric snugly around them. If you are attempting this for the first time, try to avoid tricky rooms with lots of windows, doors and other potential problems.

Tack the first panel in position and, when you're satisfied that it is straight, staple the centre point of the top edge, then the centre of the bottom edge and finally the centre of each side, pulling the fabric taut as you go. Work around the panel in this way, stapling the fabric firmly in place and removing the tacks when you feel sure that the entire panel is secure. You can then begin on the next panel. Working left to right, place the second piece of fabric almost on top of the stretched first panel with right sides together. Staple or tack down the length of the fabric so that when it is pulled across to the right, both sets of staples are hidden.

Carry on in this way until you have covered the whole area. Don't worry too much if the joints look a bit rough and ready as you can cover them with braid or cord in a contrasting colour.

- Start with plain or striped fabrics as repeats are liable to be wasteful and therefore expensive.

- This method of covering walls is especially useful for disguising plasterwork that is in a very poor state of repair.
- If you know where you'll be hanging picture and mirrors or attaching wall lights, make sure that you fix battens to support them.
- Give panels an extra-luxurious look by attaching wadding to the wall so that the stretched fabric has a slightly padded appearance.
- Make sure that you use countersunk screws for attaching the wooden battens so that the heads do not protrude and damage the fabric.

Throws

If you can't afford to re-upholster a tatty sofa and the prospect of making loose covers seems too complicated and time-consuming, a throw is the ideal solution. Throws come in many guises from blanket-like plaids to lightweight quilted prints. They may be either rectangular or square, are generously-proportioned and are designed to be draped casually over sofas and chairs. They also provide a quick cover-up if your sofa doesn't fit in with a particular colour scheme. Whatever their appearance, however, throws are extremely versatile and may be used in virtually every room in the house.

It takes a little practice to get the knack of draping and arranging throws so that they look right but it is worth the effort. Some designs are versatile enough to use as table cloths, bedspreads or even picnic rugs! And with practice, throws may also be draped and knotted round small chairs to create instant loose covers.

If you have trouble finding something suitable in the shops, many colourful rugs and lightweight quilts make good alternatives. Or you might like to try making a throw in your own fabric to co-ordinate with an existing colour scheme.

Once your throw is complete, you can drape it over the back of a sofa or chair or across the bed to provide an extra luxurious layer of comfort and warmth.

you will need

- A piece of fabric which is as long as it is wide (in this example, 1.5m (1 2/3 yds). You can use anything from heavy tapestry-like fabric to velvet or cotton.
- Co-ordinating fabric of the same dimensions for lining
- 1.5m (1 2/3 yds) lightweight wadding
- 6m (6.5 yds) fringing or other trimming
- Co-ordinating thread (if using a multi-coloured fabric, opt for the darkest shade for the thread)
- Pins and needle
- Tape measure
- Scissors

step by step
THROW

1. With right sides together, pin the main fabric to the lining. Tack.

2. Pin the wadding to the underside of the two joined pieces so that you have a square with the main fabric on top (wrong side facing you), lining in the middle and wadding at the bottom. Tack again.

3. Machine-stitch around the square leaving a seam allowance of around 3 cm (1 1/4 in). Leave a gap along one third of the length of one of the sides so that you can turn the throw right sides out.

4. Trim the excess wadding close to the seam and mitre the corners so they do not look bulky. Turn throw and close the gap with neat hand-sewing.

5. With the main fabric facing you, pin the trimming around the edge of the throw. Sew it in place by hand, taking care to turn corners neatly.

Cushions

If you have odds and ends of fabric lying in a bag, cushion covers are an ideal way of putting them to good use. There are all sorts of clever ideas for covers from designs with flat-edged trims to those with neat button fastenings. But if sewing is an anathema to you, you can still use those remnants to cover cushions every bit as stylishly as hand-sewn designs.

Patterned cushions
heaped on a sofa
create an air of
opulence. These
designs in spice
colours are inspired by
ethnic patterns such as
those found on kelims
and Paisley shawls.

Bolster cushions make a wonderful finishing touch placed at either end of a sofa. For an instant bolster cover, simply roll a length of fabric around the cushion, leaving at least 15 cm (6 in) fabric at either end. With a length of cord, tie the fabric at each end so that the 'sausage' has two tails. You could either use quite opulent cord and leave the knotted end as a decorative detail or, if you opt for a plainer cord, you can add one or two tassels for a luxurious look.

Experiment with different cords and trims on a variety of fabrics. When you get fed up with the cover you can simply undo it and start again. If the tail ends of fabric fray or begin to look messy, just trim the edges with a pair of pinking shears.

You can cheat when covering more conventionally-shaped cushions too. With a little careful wrapping, you'll be able to secure 'covers' with cord, tassels and ribbon tied into bows.

PVC Tablecloth

Nothing could be simpler to make than this PVC tablecloth. Perfect for garden tables and summer barbecues, the cloth would also make an attractive cover for a kitchen table. If you don't have time for sewing, you can simply cut the PVC with scissors or pinking shears to fit your table – the plastic coating means that it will not fray. For a neater edge, simply turn up a small hem and stick or machine-stitch it all round.

you will need

- PVC fabric
- Scissors
  or
  Pinking shears
- Tape measure
- Suitable glue
- Iron
- Protective cloth

step by step PVC TABLECLOTH

1. Measure the length and breadth of your table. The fabric used here is 120cm (48in) wide which should be wide enough for most garden tables. Measure down one leg of the table to see how much of a drop you'd like. (If your table is very wide you may have to use double the width of fabric – see note for details.)

2. Add the length of the table top and twice the drop, plus 4cm (1 1/2 in) for hem allowances. This gives you the complete length of the fabric needed. Add the width of the tabletop and twice the drop, plus 4cm (1 1/2in) for the width needed.

3. Cut the fabric to the size you have decided on, then turn under 2cm (3/4in) all round. Press the hem into position using a cloth between your iron and the PVC and stick it down using the recommended glue.

Note If you are using a double width of fabric, a seam down the middle of the cloth is rather unattractive. Divide the second width into two, lengthways, and make the joins along each side of the table top. Make a plan of your measurements and draw in the position of each join, with seam allowances, before you start cutting.

STEP 1

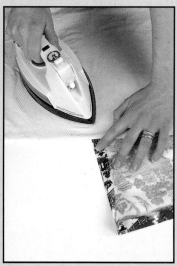

STEP 2

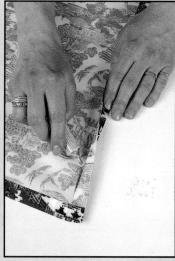

STEP 3

*A plastic-coated
tablecloth like this
could not be easier to
make and is a practical
addition to any kitchen.
PVC comes in a
wonderful range of
patterns and colours.*

*In fresh shades of pink
and green, these floral
chair covers look
irresistibly pretty. For
a totally different look,
you could try making
them in calico or smart
ticking stripes.*

Chair Covers

Second-hand chairs are usually cheap and easy to come by. It is worth not only scouring charity and second-hand shops but looking out for auctions too. These pretty covers will transform the plainest designs into attractive dining or occasional chairs. Use different patterns to give each chair its own look or sew a matching set for a more formal and co-ordinated look. The wood can be painted to match the fabric.

you will need

Covers:
- Paper for making templates. Dressmaker's pattern-cutting paper (available from the haberdashery department of good department stores) is marked with a grid that makes measuring easier, but you could also use large sheets of brown paper or greaseproof paper.
- Suitable furnishing fabric. The amount you need depends on the size of your chair (and on whether you're making a cushion or full cover) – see instructions below for estimating fabric, and measure the chair carefully before you buy.
- Covered piping cord (optional). This can be chosen to match or contrast with the fabric you are using – either way, it will add a really professional finish.

Cushion:
- A sheet of 5cm (2in) thick furnishing foam the size of the chair seat. If your foam is a different thickness, adjust the fabric measurements in the estimating and making instructions accordingly.

FRILLED CUSHION COVER

To estimate fabric:

- First measure the chair seat's dimensions. If you're using 5cm (2in) deep foam, add 6cm (2 1/2in) to each side, ie 12cm (5 in) to total measurements from side to side and front to back, to allow for cushion depth plus 1cm (1/2in) seam allowance. (Adapt this calculation if you're using a different thickness of foam.)
- Decide on the depth of the frill you'd like and add an extra 2cm (3/4in) to this measurement for seam and hem. Add up the lengths of the two sides and front of the cushion cover (eg 33cm + 33cm + 40cm = 106cm/13in + 13in + 15 3/4in = 41 3/4in), then add half that figure again to allow for gathering (eg 106cm + 53cm = 159cm/ 14 3/4in + 21in = 62 3/4in) plus 2cm (3/4in) for seams. If you need to economize on fabric, the frill can be made in three pieces, joined at front corners – each piece should be 1 1/2 times the relevant length, plus 2cm (3/4in) for seams.
- To make the cushion ties, cut four strips of fabric 36 x 4cm (14 x 1 1/2in) each.

step by step CUSHIONS

1. Make a paper template of the chair, adding 6cm (2 1/2in) on all sides (as shown in diagram). Cut fabric to this larger size and mark position of the seat corners with threads. Use the template to cut out foam to the exact size and shape of the seat.

2. Press corners of the fabric diagonally from each thread mark to corner point. Mark fabric at the point 6cm (2 1/2in) along outside edge from each of the corners (see diagram).

3. Sew between each thread and 6cm (2 1/2in) edge marking and trim off excess fabric (as shown in diagram). These seams form the corners of the cover to fit over the foam cushion.

4. If you're using three sections of fabric to form the frill, sew them together, then hem the lower long edge and short ends of frill fabric. Sew running stitch through the top long edge and gather to the exact length to fit round the front and two sides of the cushion, then machine stitch through the gather to secure.

5. If you are using piping cord, machine stitch it to the right side of the fabric around the side and front edges, making sure you keep the rough edge of the fabric aligned with the raw edge of the piping.

6. Sew on the frill around the front and side edges of the cushion cover, ensuring that the piping remains visible on the right side.

7. Hem the back edge of the cover.

8. Make ties. Hem short ends of each fabric strip. Fold in both long edges by 1cm (1/2in), then fold each strip in on itself again and stick as close to the edge as possible (see diagram).

9. Sew two ties to each side of cover at back to attach cushion to chair.

10. Press all seams flat, fit cover over foam cushion and tie to chair.

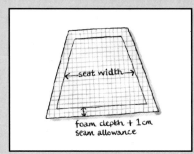

seat width

foam depth + 1cm seam allowance

STEP 1

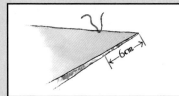

6cm

STEP 2

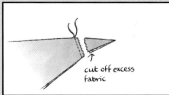

cut off excess fabric

STEP 3

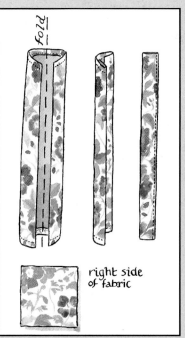

fold

right side of fabric

STEP 8

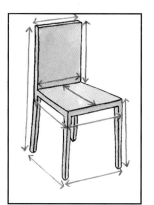

TIE-ON CHAIR COVER

This style works best with square-topped upright chairs, so is ideal for giving old-fashioned dining chairs a new lease of life.

To estimate fabric:

- Take the chair's measurements as shown in the diagram and draw up a plan on graph paper. Try to measure it at as many points as possible, as there may be some variations from front to back and side to side.
- Use these measurements to work out the dimensions of the main front, back and side pieces, as shown in the diagram. If your fabric doesn't have an obvious one-way pattern, you can use a single long piece to combine the back and front of the cover. Add 1cm (1/2in) extra all round for seams and hems.
- For facings on opening edges, allow for four strips of fabric 12cm (4 3/4in) wide, each the same length as the chair's full back height (as in diagram) plus 2cm (3/4in) for seams and hems.
- Decide on the number, length and thickness of ties you'll need for fastening the cover over the chair. Here 16 strips 8 x 42cm (3 x 16in) have been sewn up to make 3 x 40 cm (1 1/4 x 15in) ties, but there are numerous alternatives. For example, you may prefer three bold bows on each side or ten pairs of lace-thin ties for a more delicate effect, or ribbons to match the piping.

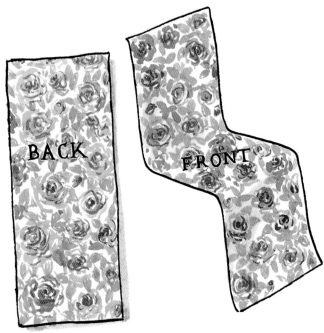

BACK

FRONT

SIDE

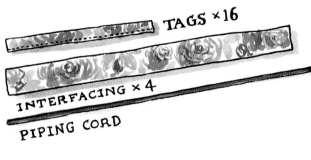

TAGS ×16

INTERFACING × 4

PIPING CORD

step by step TIE-ON CHAIR COVER

STEP 3

right side of fabric

STEP 4

1. Make paper templates for the various pieces of chair cover as estimated and cut out fabric.

2. If you have cut back and front pieces separately, sew them together along top edge. If you are using piping cord, sew it on the right side of the fabric along long edges of front and back, aligning the rough edge of the cord with raw edge of the fabric.

3. Join side panels to front piece as shown in the diagram, taking care to sew as close to the piping cord as possible. Trim seams.

4. The main body of the cover is now ready for you to add ties and facing. To make ties, fold in a 1cm (1/2in) hem on each long edge, fold in half lengthways again, and topstitch together as close to the edge as possible (see diagram).

5. Sew the front and back facings together along short top edges to make two long strips (see left), and hem one long edge of each.

6. Tack ties securely in place at regular intervals down the right side of the main body of the cover, as shown in the diagram.

7. Pin and sew facing to the right side of fabric, securing the ties at the same time.

8. Press seams and fold facing inside. Hem lower edges, and handstitch facing along hem edge to secure. Trim any excess fabric and press thoroughly.

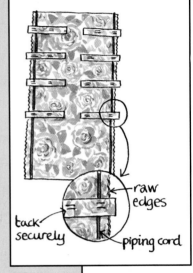

raw edges

tack securely

piping cord

STEP 6

sew   sew

STEP 7

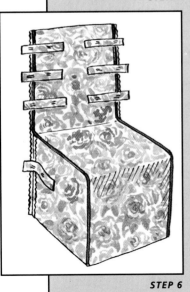

STEP 6

Fabric Headboard

The plainest divan bed can be transformed with a fabric-covered headboard. Anything from smart stripes and checks to pretty floral patterns are suitable and you could even choose coloured bedlinen to co-ordinate.

- Sheet of 1cm (1/2in) chipboard, measuring 140cm (4ft 6in) (or the width of your bed) x 90cm (3ft).
- Pair of headboard fixings to attach to the board so it can be slotted on to your divan. Alternatively, mount the headboard on to the wall behind the bed.
- Thick wadding (the kind used for quilting) measuring 2.8m x 90cm (109 x 36in). If the wadding feels too thin, allow double the amount.
- Heavy duty staple gun, tin tacks and hammer or strong glue to attach the wadding to the board.
- Around 3 1/2sq.m(4sq.yds) of fabric – see step 1 for more details
- Press studs or Velcro (optional)

Why not make a headboard to co-ordinate with your favourite bedlinen? Red and blue checks teamed with smart chambray and paisley-patterned sheets make a stylish combination.

step by step FABRIC HEADBOARD

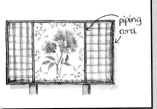

STEP 1

1. You need two pieces of 152 x 100cm (60 x 39in) fabric to work with, so ideally you should choose fabric 152cm (60in) wide to avoid visible joins. If the fabric is narrower, its length will run from left to right rather than top to bottom, so choose a non-directional pattern. If you cannot avoid joining smaller pieces together to make up the size, you could make a feature of the seams by covering them with piping or bias binding in a contrasting colour.

2. Cover board with wadding, sewing or stapling the ends together at the back. Tack or staple it to the board, or use a suitable glue.

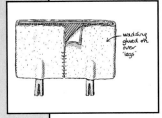

STEP 2

3. After making any joins needed (see Step 1), sew the two pieces of 152 x 100cm (60 x 39in) fabric together along one long edge as shown in the diagram.

4. Hem the top and bottom edges of the fabric. You now have two options. You can either stitch the sides of the doubled-over fabric together as in the diagram, leaving only the bottom seam open to create a sleeve which will pull over the board, or you can finish the two outer edges with hems and attach ties (as in the photograph) to fix the sides together with bows down the outside edges of the board. Whichever method you choose, the cover should fit snugly so that the wadding gives the board a softly rounded look.

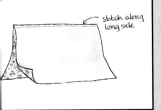

STEP 3

5. Carefully press all seams, then turn the cover right side out.

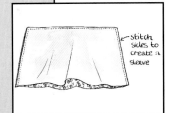

STEP 4

6. To make the ties, cut strips of matching or contrasting fabric each 38 x 7.5cm (15 x 3in). Choose a lightweight fabric or the bows will be difficult to tie neatly. Hem the short ends, then fold the long sides in on themselves so there are no raw edges, and sew along the long edge to make a strip 2.5cm (1in) wide.

7. Sew the ties to the cover edges, making sure they are equally spaced and that both sides match. The example here uses ten bows (five on each side) but you can use a different number if you like.

STEP 7

8. To secure the lower edges of the cover, use press studs, Velcro or additional ties – it needs to be easily removable for washing or dry-cleaning.

*Turn your bed into
something from a
fairytale by fixing a
canopy above it. This
one is lined in plain
chintz but you could
use a pattern like a
stripe for a more
dramatic effect.*

OTHER BRIGHT IDEAS FOR HEADBOARDS

- Use a plain chintz, and add piped edges and bows in a contrasting colour.
- Applique your own design onto a plain fabric cover – fun shapes make an ideal headboard for a child's room.
- Sew on contrasting ribbon or strips of plain or patterned fabric to add a decorative border.
- Paint or stencil a design onto plain canvas or calico using fabric paints and continue the pattern in emulsion on the wall behind the bed for a co-ordinated look.

BRIGHT IDEAS FOR SHEETS

- Tiny buttons look chic sewn along the edge of a pillowcase. Don't worry about buttonholes – the buttons don't have to work, just look decorative.
- Add a contrasting strip of fabric to the top of a sheet and decorate the seam with ric-rac braid or plain binding.
- Lace and broderie anglais can transform the plainest sheets and pillowcases. Gather a wide length to trim outside edges or use narrower designs to decorate the seam dividing two different prints.

CHAPTER FIVE

WOOD AND TILES

In this informal bathroom, tongue and groove has been fitted to dado height and then painted blue. Although this bath is freestanding, some designs could be panelled with tongue and groove to match.

Don't be put off using these versatile materials. Even if you are new to DIY, there are all sorts of clever kits and tricks around which help you to get the most out of wood and tiles. If you can wield a hammer and a saw, you'll find many DIY projects are a great deal simpler than you would have ever expected.

Wood

ARCHITECTURAL FEATURES

Many modern homes and older properties which have been unlovingly 'modernised' lack the architectural features that lend so much character and interest. Dado rails, picture rails and decorative panels are simple to reinstate by using lengths of moulding, often based on original designs. Try to make sure you choose a design that is appropriate for the age and style of your home. Make a note of the dimensions of the room and, if in doubt, try to borrow samples before you make a decision.

If you live in a brand new home with no existing architectural features, however, you have a free hand in deciding which styles you'd like to use.

WOODEN PANELLING

Whether you prefer the simplicity of a tongue and groove dado or floor to ceiling panelling reminiscent of a baronial banqueting hall, wooden cladding provides instant coverage for walls. Wooden panelling is available in a variety of styles and may be used to provide quick coverage for interior walls. With the correct choice of panelling you can give your home the look of a Tudor or Georgian property.

Tongue and groove panelling lends an informal, cottagey feel to rooms and tends to work best in small to medium-sized areas. The wooden strips come in standard widths which simply slot together – hence the name – and are attached to wooden battens nailed to the wall. Although tongue and groove is commonly used vertically to make a panelled dado, it may also be fixed horizontally from floor to ceiling to create the impression of a weatherboarded beach house. (If you do fix the boards horizontally, make sure that you fix the battens to the wall vertically so that they run at right angles and provide a secure framework.) Also known as matchboarding, tongue and groove is often sold in packs of ready-cut lengths which makes it easier to work with if you're not experienced in handling tools.

Once in situ, the panelling may be stained or painted to co-ordinate with any colour scheme. A useful way of disguising damaged walls, tongue and groove (or any wooden panelling for that matter) should never be used to cover damp.

DADO RAILS

Sometimes known as chair rails, dado rails run at around the height of a chair back. They divide the wall in two and provide a lot of scope for combining different papers and paints above and below. The dado (lower level) may be clad in a variety of materials from tongue and groove to panels made from wooden mouldings.

MOULDED PANELLING FOR ROOMS

This idea can be used on a grander scale to create panels within a room. Plot the

This wood panelling has been painted a soft shade of yellow to give it a contemporary look.

dimensions on a piece of paper and plan how you want to lay the panels out before you start cutting the wood. Again, it's far easier to paint, stain or varnish the

mouldings before they are in situ. You can create different effects by using two shades of paint – one on the main wall and one within the panels.

DOOR PANELS

Modern doors can look somewhat feature-less if simply painted. If you yearn for a period-style panelled door, it's remarkably easy to transform a flush door with mouldings mitred and tacked into four or six panels. Kits are available in DIY sheds and stores which made the task even quicker and simpler.

step by step
DOOR PANELS

1. Make sure the surface of the door is clean and completely free from dust.

2. Decide how many panels you want to use and where to place. Look at books, magazines and original panelled doors if you need good reference material.

3. Mitre the mouldings into lengths to make up the requisite squares and/or rectangles. Fix them at the corners by nailing in corrugated clips (available from good art suppliers and DIY stores). If you are going to paint or varnish the mouldings, you'll find it much easier to do it at this stage.

4. Having marked the site of the panels on the door with pencil, position each one carefully. Use a spirit level to ensure the top and bottom mouldings are horizontal. Also make sure that panels are at exactly the same height. Mouldings from kits are often ready-coated with adhesive so simply peel away the backing strips before pressing them into place. If you are not using a kit, coat the mouldings with wood adhesive, according to the manufacturer's instructions, and secure with fine tacks.

Sanding a Floor

If your floorboards are in reasonably good condition, you may want to hire a sander to take them back to their original state before sealing them with stain or varnish. Sanded floors look attractive left bare or covered with richly patterned kelims and rugs, and the range of stains and varnishes available means that you don't have to stick to a natural wood finish.

There is a knack to using an upright sander as they have a tendency to run away with you! If you hire one for the weekend you should have time to get to grips with it and, if you persevere, you will find the job is not actually very difficult. It is very messy, however, so do all you can to minimise the amount of dust settling!

Preparation

- Hammer down all protruding nail heads so that they do not catch on the sandpaper.
- Fill in any gaps with slivers of wood glued into place.
- Using steel wool and white spirit, remove any traces of old polish.
- Hammer down any loose floorboards so they are firmly in position.
- Open windows and tape the gaps between the door and frame to minimise the amount of dust settling.

SAFETY NOTES

- You *must* wear a mask, ear muffs and goggles.
- Make sure that the flex is always kept well clear of the machine's path.
- Always turn the machine off and disconnect it from the mains when you are changing the paper.
- If you intend to put down carpets or rugs, buy grips so that they do not slip on the newly-sanded surface.

step by step
SANDING A FLOOR

1. Start with a coarse grade paper and fit it to the machine according to the manual or operating instructions. Whenever you need to change paper, make sure that the machine is switched off and disconnected.

2. Sand diagonally across the boards at an angle of 45 degrees, tilting the machine at the beginning and end of each row.

3. When you have completed the diagonals, fit medium grade paper to the sander and work up and down the boards along the grain of the wood.

4. With fine grade paper fitted to the sander, work up and down along the grain of the wood once again.

5. Using an edging sander, sand the edges of the room that could not be reached by the main machine. Keep working along the grain of the wood.

6. Finish any small areas that you might have missed by hand and then leave the room overnight to allow dust to settle.

7. Vacuum the floor (if your machine does not have an integral vacuum, it's worth doing this throughout the process).

8. Wipe down the boards with white spirit then apply stain or varnish according to the manufacturer's instructions.

Tiled Surfaces

Tiles come in a huge variety of styles and designs ranging from rough-hewn ethnic designs to up-to-the-minute contemporary patterns. There are even reproductions of traditional Victorian and Edwardian tiles so that you can recreate an authentic period-style atmosphere.

If you've never tried tiling a wall before, you'll be surprised at how straightforward a task it is. Like so many other projects, it is important to be well prepared before you start work.

Before you start

- Walls must be dry. Damp patches should be treated and new plaster allowed to dry thoroughly.
- Old wallpaper and flaking paint should be removed. If the painted surface is in good condition, roughen the surface with coarse grade sandpaper to give the tiles a grip.
- Plasterwork must be in good condition. Replace any crumbly patches.
- If a wall is already covered in tiles you can tile a new layer directly on top rather than chip them all off. Make sure that the old tiles are clean, then roughen the surface with a scriber.
- If you plan to place one layer of tiles on top of another, position the new tiles so that the lines of grouting do not coincide.
- To calculate how many tiles you will need, multiply the width of the area to be covered by its height to give you the square metreage or yardage. It's wise to add at least 5 per cent to this figure to allow for breakages. Most packs of tiles provide information on the area they will cover. If in doubt, ask the sales assistant.
- To avoid colour variation, try to ensure that all tiles are from the same batch.
- If you are going to mix patterned and plain tiles, plot the design on squared paper before you start.
- On a plain wall, try to ensure that the cut tiles at either end are the same size.
- If there is a window in the wall, make it a focal point. Draw a vertical line through its centre on the wall and tile outwards from there.

---

step by step **TILING**

1. Nail a straight wooden batten along the wall, one tile depth above the skirting board. Use a spirit level to ensure it is horizontal.

2. With a notched spreader, coat the wall above the batten with a layer of adhesive. Work an area of around one square metre (yard) at a time.

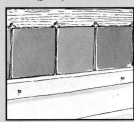

3. Fix the tiles to the wall, pressing them into the adhesive to ensure that they are well stuck. The bottom edge of the tile should rest against the top of the batten.

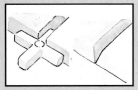

4. Working along the batten, fix the tiles to the wall, inserting plastic spacers as you go to ensure the grouting will be even.

5. The spacers should be pressed in below the level of the tiles so that the grout will cover them.

6. Leave gaps at the end of the row for the time being. Work upwards until you have a few rows.

7. To cut tiles to fit the end gaps, measure the space to be filled with a steel measuring tape and transfer the measurement to the glazed side of the tile. Mark with a pen. With

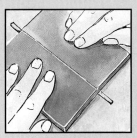

a scriber, score along the line so that the glaze is cut. Place two matchsticks under the tile, one at either end of the score mark. Press down gently and the tile should snap cleanly in two. You will probably find it easier to use a tile cutter to transfer the shape of the gap on to the tile.

8. With a file or abrasive paper, smooth the cut edge before placing it in position. Always file away from the glaze.

Tiles can be used not merely to cover walls but to frame windows and delineate separate areas of a room. Co-ordinated collections like the one shown here make it easy to mix several different patterns with plain tiles.

TILED BORDERS

Border tiles provide the icing on the cake. They come in different designs ranging from narrow pencil-like relief edging to deep borders which are often highly patterned.

- When tiling around kitchen splashback, make sure the border tiles are positioned at least one tile down from the top row so that kitchen cupboards do not obscure them.
- If the space you are tiling has a high ceiling, use a row of border tiles about one third of the way down the wall to give the illusion of a lower ceiling.
- Once you become adept at tiling, you can use tiles to create panelled shapes within a wall of tiles.

MURAL TILES

Although expensive, mural tiles are a stunning means of creating a focal point on a tiled surface. When positioned, they form a large scale picture or scene so are an ideal way of decorating areas behind the hob or bath. They may be used in conjunction with patterned and plain tiles but it is best to keep the look quite restrained so that the mural makes more of an impact.

RELIEF TILES

A perfect means of introducing textural interest without necessarily adding more colour, relief tiles look particularly effective when used in borders or dotted about amongst flat tiles.

- The occasional relief tile can add depth to a plain tiled surface whether it is a single colour or a combination of different shades.
- Combine flat and relief-patterned tiles decorated with the same motif.

While they are expensive to replace, you can make the most of existing tiles in several ways. Grout, for example, tends to be taken for granted, but if coloured will transform the appearance of wall tiles. There are transfers available which are designed to be stuck on to existing plain surfaces to create instant decor tiles and you can even use paint to cover unattractive ceramic tiles.

PAINTING TILES

Use eggshell or gloss paint to cover ceramic tiles. You can create paint effects like sponging and ragging if you want a more textured effect.

step by step
PAINTING TILES

1. With methylated spirit, wipe the tiled surface dry. If the tiles you wish to cover are patterned, coat the area with white gloss paint.

2. For the ragged base coat, mix 3 parts gloss or eggshell paint with 7 parts transparent oil glaze. Thin with white spirit and paint on to tiles.

3. Whilst paint is wet, roll a cotton rag on the surface to give a subtly shaded effect. Then leave to dry.

4. Make a square-shaped stencil, using a tile as a template. Coat an offcut of wood or board with the second colour and 'charge' a sea sponge with the paint. Position the stencil carefully and sponge. Move the stencil around and continue sponging until the all-over pattern is complete.

HINTS FOR USING TILES

- Tiles of different designs can be mixed together if they are a similar colour.
- A multi-coloured mosaic of tiles can be set between two parallel rows of border tiles.
- Mirror tiles are a good way to accentuate space and are useful in small bathrooms and hallways.
- Tiled worktops are practical next to hobs and ovens. They provide an ideal heat-resistant surface for pans and dishes.

Screens

Hinged screens, made from solid wooden panels or frames covered in fabric, are a useful way of creating instant, temporary partitions. In smaller homes they are invaluable for delineating specific areas within a room: you can, for example, create a dining area within a living room or kitchen simply by pulling a screen alongside the table. Small scale screens provide a novel means of disguising unsightly radiators. The screen panels themselves may be shaped with curved, angled or even Gothic-style pointed tops.

Solid wooden panels may be decorated in a number of ways to co-ordinate with any scheme. Anything from simple paint effects to elaborate découpage are effective methods and are easy to achieve. You could even attempt a small-scale print room by sticking prints or photocopies on to panels which have been painted or papered. Screens are an ideal size for trying out techniques such as stencilling before you feel confident enough to translate them to larger-scale projects.

Fabric-covered screens come in two basic designs. In one, the fabric is stretched tightly across the frame to give a flat surface; with the other, it is gathered at the top and bottom of the frame, giving a soft draped appearance. Most furnishing fabrics are suitable for use on the frame of a screen but if it is to be pulled tight, make sure that the cloth is quite tough. Gathered fabric, on the other hand, should be fairly soft so that it ruches easily and does not appear bulky or bunched.

FRETWORK

These finely carved wooden panels are reminiscent of Turkish or Far Eastern architecture. Ideal for making partitions, fretwork allows light to filter through from one area to another while maintaining a degree of screened privacy. Several panels can be hinged together. Fretwork panels can also be cut to add interesting effects to ceilings and walls.

*A plain canvas-covered
screen is the ideal
basis for painted
designs. This hand-
painted chequerboard
pattern looks stunning
and is relatively easy to
achieve.*

step by step
PAINTED SCREEN

you will need

- Eight 150cm (5ft) lengths of 5 x 2.5cm (2 x 1in) wood
- Eight 36cm (14in) long pieces of 15 x 2.5cm (6 x 1in) wood
- Measuring tape
- Jigsaw
- Drill
- Wood glue
- 32 x 7.5cm (3in) screws
- Screwdriver
- Canvas or heavyweight calico – enough to cover four frames, each measuring 150cm (5ft) tall x 46cm (18in) wide, and with 5cm (2in) to spare all around
- Heavy-duty staple gun
- Emulsion paint – 1 litre each of the two colours you are using for the chequerboard pattern.
- Pencil and ruler
- Six brass hinges, about 5cm (2in) long (with screws)
- Masking tape (optional)
- Upholstery braid (optional)

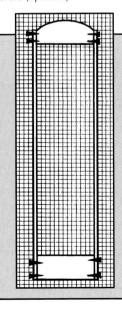

1. *Each panel is a frame made from four pieces of wood. The two uprights are 150cm (5ft) lengths of 5 x 2.5cm (2 x 1in) and the top and base are made from 36cm (14in) lengths of 15 x 2.5cm (6 x 1in). Most timber merchants are happy to cut wood to size for you.*

2. *To create the rounded top of the screen, you need to cut the top piece of 15 x 2.5cm (6 x 1in) into a semi-circle, as shown in diagram.*

3. *Lay all the cut pieces out flat on the floor, with the top and base pieces on the inside of the uprights. Mark the position of screw holes on all pieces and drill through. Position screws as shown in the diagram, using two on either side top and bottom (ie eight screws per panel). Use a countersink bit on the drill to provide the shaped hole necessary to allow the screws to sit flush with the surface once screwed in place.*

4. *Squeeze wood glue on to the faces that touch and then twist the screws home. Leave glue to dry.*

5. *Cut the canvas into four pieces, each one measuring 162 x 56cm (5ft 4in x 22in).*

continued overleaf

6. Lay the first piece of canvas or calico on top of its frame, tuck round edge of frame and begin to staple into place, fastening to rear. The canvas should not be stretched too tightly as it will shrink a little when the paint begins to dry – allow it a bit of give without letting it wrinkle. Staple the canvas three or four times in the middle of one of the uprights, then stretch the canvas across and do the same on the other side. Attach canvas to the top and bottom in the same way. Note: you could cover both sides of the screen – just double the amount of canvas.

7. Once the canvas is firmly in place, staple along the remaining edges until you come to the corners. These should be turned under neatly and stapled. Treat all four panels in this way.

8. Now you are ready to paint the screen. Coat each panel with the paler of your two colours and leave to dry.

9. Make sure the panels are laid side by side in sequence so that you can begin your design. Use a pencil and ruler to mark out the chequerboard pattern as shown in the diagram.

10. Paint the diamonds in the second colour. The pattern shown here has been painted freehand, which leaves the edges looking slightly uneven but you can use masking tape to achieve a more defined line. Leave to dry.

11. To finish off the edges of the panels you can add some upholstery braid. This can be attached with glue, staples or upholstery tacks.

12. To join the panels, lay them in sequence (painted side up) ready to attach the hinges. Using two hinges to join each pair of panels, join the outer panels to their adjacent ones first. To attach the last pair of hinges, turn panels over to face the floor, and screw the hinges on to the wrong side. This allows the screen to be folded concertina-fashion.

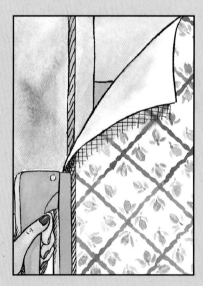

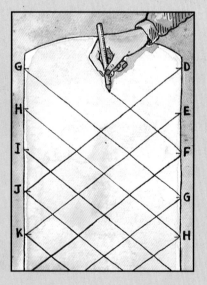

WOODEN SCREEN

If you prefer, you can make a screen from solid panels of MDF (medium-density fibreboard) or plywood rather than a covered frame. MDF is fairly heavy so while the screen will certainly be sturdy, it will not be easy to move around. If it is important that your screen is portable, stick to the lighter weight version comprising frame and covering.

Timber merchants usually sell sheets of wood in standard sizes and while 244 x 122cm (8 x 4ft) is a common measurement, it is not ideal for making a screen. You will need to cut panels measuring 152cm (5ft)

tall x 46cm (18in) wide so try to find sheets of MDF or plywood which measure 182 x 90cm (6 x 3ft) overall – that way you will manage to cut four panels from two sheets with little wastage.

As an alternative to MDF you could use plywood which, though lighter, does not have the same smooth finish. You may find that it takes longer to achieve a professional-looking paint finish on plywood, but there are other options for decorating the screen which might be more appropriate. You might like to try a distressed paint finish or perhaps have a go at a découpage or stencilling.

---

step by step
ATTACHING HINGES TO PANELS

you will need

- Two sheets of 1cm (1/2in) thick MDF or plywood
- Six hinges or screws measuring around 4cm (1 1/2 in) long x 2.5cm (1in) wide – each of the flat side plates with screw holes should be no more than 1cm (1/2 in) so they fit neatly on the panel (if you are leaving them unpainted, brass hinges look best)
- Screwdriver
- Drill
- 2cm (3/4in) chisel
- Saw
- Workbench or solid surface to support the sheets of wood
- Metal G clamps to hold the wood steady
- Measuring tape
- Pencil
- Rule or straight edge

For a neat finish, the hinges can be rebated (recessed) as follows:

1. Draw around the shape of the hinge plates in position and begin to chisel away the area. Don't chisel any further than the depth of the hinges – it is better to err on the side of caution and fix the hinges slightly proud of the surface.

2. The drill bit should be slightly smaller than the screws you are using so that the screw threads will be able to get a good grip as you twist them into the pilot hole.

3. Drill your pilot hole slightly shallower than the length of the screw.

4. Remember to fix sets of hinges so that the screen folds in a concertina fashion (see step 12 on facing page).

CHAPTER SIX

ACCESSORIES AND DISPLAY

BELOW *A collection of small framed pictures and photographs, hooks and even tiny scissors makes an unusual decorative display.*

RIGHT *Everything from old enamel advertising boards, to posters and gilt letters from shop signs have been used to create an eclectic gallery that is quite unique.*

No matter what your budget or the style of your home, carefully chosen and displayed accessories can make the difference between a sterile showhouse and a home which reflects your taste and personality. No matter how tasteful a colour scheme or how well decorated your home, it will never have a true identity unless you make your mark in this way.

Pictures and Prints

You don't have to own a collection of Old Masters to enjoy works of art. And while there are many good reasons for investing in

original paintings and prints, with a little imagination and flair you can transform even a humble collection of postcards into an exciting gallery in your own home.

Small pictures and prints tend to get lost when hung on a bare wall on their own – for maximum effect, the pictures should be grouped together. Don't worry about matching the frames – a mixture of different styles will usually work just as well. If at first you don't feel confident about arranging groups of pictures, stick to using frames of a single finish such as gilt or wood. You might like to introduce some variety by making sure there is a good mixture of interesting textures ranging from simple mouldings to ornately carved wood. This textural contrast is a useful way of adding depth to any collection of similar items, whether picture frames or cushions. As you gain confidence, you'll find it easier to combine frames and pictures in a wider variety of different styles and materials. The beauty of it is that nothing has to be a permanent fixture. If you don't like the position of a picture or you just get fed up with it, you can change it straight away.

Mixed groups of pictures can have a formal or informal air, depending on how you choose to hang them. A symmetrical arrangement will look more formal than a random collection of pictures.

Once you have got the knack of putting pictures in position, there are many accessories available which will help to make

An antique map, framed painting and oval mirror swathed in a garland of ivy prove an unusually successful trio.

a feature of a painting or group of pictures.

Picture bows so beloved by the Victorians are a popular means of decorating pictures and mirrors too. Most commonly made from chintz or moire, the bows are tacked in position above a painting with their tails appearing below its bottom edge. The weight of the picture is not borne by the bow, although it gives that impression. Bows may come with a single or double 'tail'. A long single tail is an ideal way of displaying groups of framed prints or cameos in a row, as it provides a strong link. Picture bows displaying a group of small prints look very effective in small corners or narrow spaces where they add a sense of purpose and prevent the pictures from getting lost. They also look very smart hung fairly low on either side of a fireplace where the pictures may be enjoyed by anyone seated nearby. Picture rosettes are like picture bows but the tails are topped with a frilled rosette rather than a bow.

You can also create trompe l'oeil picture bows by stencilling or painting directly on to the wall.

Cord is another similar method for adorning walls and is especially useful for bringing coherence to groups of pictures. Picture cord may be tied into decorative knots which provide a display of pictures with a focal point. The cord itself is more flexible than the tails of a picture bow and may be swagged across a group of pictures and tied into another knot before hanging down. Some skill is required to get the hang of using picture cord but kits are available which give details on how to get the best results.

Decorative hooks come in many designs to appeal to all tastes. For classical rooms there are garlands, stars and fleurs de lys, while more lighthearted motifs such as bees and mice are also popular. Although small in scale, details like this do not go unnoticed and it can be fun trying to find an image that is appropriate for the framed picture.

Pegs and Hooks

Ideal for small areas, hooks and pegs may be used to display both practical and decorative bits and pieces. Kitchens, with all their paraphernalia, need as much storage space as possible but if your cupboards are overflowing, you can make an attractive feature of seemingly mundane accessories such as pots and pans.

One of the easiest (and handiest) ways of using hooks is to fit a chrome or brass rail just below kitchen wall cupboards. Small hooks are sold with these rails and may be used for suspending colanders, sieves, whisks or even bunches of herbs. If you do have to store things in the open, make a feature of them rather than apologize for their existence.

Suspended from the ceiling, racks are another means of hanging kitchen tools and implements and they often make decorative features in their own right. They come in a variety of designs and materials so whether you want a medieval-style model in wrought iron or a contemporary design in gleaming chrome, you should find one to suit your kitchen.

The benefit of having so many bits and pieces on display is that they are close at hand when you need them. But you can make the display purely decorative if you prefer: traditional pulleys, for example, are just as likely these days to be festooned with bunches of dried flowers as airing laundry!

Pegboards are a Shaker invention and were used not only to hang clothing but household goods such as brooms and candleholders. Even bulkier items like cupboards and shelves were suspended in this way. Pegboards based on original Shaker designs may be bought today. The wooden boards, with pegs spaced at regular intervals, are fixed around the wall and make feature of storage space. The key to success is the simplicity of Shaker design but you can modify the idea for use in almost any room in the home to provide accessible and stylish storage solutions.

Old-fashioned kitchen pulleys look wonderful decorated with bunches of dried flowers and herbs.

Made from beaten metal, these painted animal hooks not only look charming but are useful for storing strings of garlic and bunches of herbs.

- Use a pegboard in bathrooms for towels and spongebags.
- In the hallway or corridor for keeping coats and jackets off the floor.
- Fix at a lower level in children's rooms so they can make a colourful display and keep their rooms tidy by hanging everything up.

Even the plainest cup hooks can be used to create unusual displays. If you collect small jugs, for example, you can hang them around a doorway or in rows on a wall to make an instant feature.

Display Shelves and Stands

If you collect anything from teapots to teddy bears, it's satisfying to be able to display them together in a group where they will make far more of an impression. However objects of different shapes and sizes can present a problem.

Dressers and wall-mounted pine shelves are a perfect way of displaying collections of crockery. However, if you only have a selection of one or two plates they could be hung on the wall and embellished with picture bows. Collections of ceramics also look good when displayed on a plate shelf running round the room at the same height as a picture rail, though smaller and more delicate pieces may not be seen.

Furniture has been specially designed to house collections of smaller accessories such as keys or teaspoons. As well as small wall-mounted racks, tiny accessories may be encased in a glass-topped table where they can be clearly seen and where they are protected too.

Make a pinboard to hold souvenirs such as postcards, menus, tickets and theatre programmes. Simply cover a rectangle of chipboard with a layer of cork or wadding. Then, with a staple gun, fix a layer of felt over the wood and wadding. Secure contrasting braid or tape in a lattice pattern across the board with the staple gun, securing crossover points with a brass tack, and attach picture rings to the back for hanging.

Add interest to plain shelves with a scalloped edge cut from paper. You can use anything from old newspaper to wallpaper lining. Alternatively, add strips of lace for a pretty, country effect. Use small shelves at staggered intervals against a plain wall to add interest and provide storage space too.

Home Fragrance

An important but often neglected element when it comes to creating a welcoming home environment is scent. Estate agents have been telling us for years that there's nothing like the aroma of freshly-ground coffee beans or newly-baked bread for creating a welcoming atmosphere, yet it's very easy to take your sense of smell for granted. Of course you don't have to have a pot of fresh coffee brewing all the time, but there are many ways of introducing subtle scents to your home that are both evocative and attractive.

Fragrances have a tremendous ability to evoke memories. Pine or cinnamon-based mixtures are reminiscent of Christmas while fresh, flowery scents are evocative of spring meadows. You can even recreate the smell of the seaside in your own bathroom should the whim take you! Most home fragrances are relatively inexpensive and can be changed to suit your mood.

Pot pourri is perhaps the most popular of all home fragrances. Not only does it provide a subtle scent, it serves the double function of looking decorative, too. Gone are the

Hanging from Shaker-style pegs like these, kitchen equipment is always close at hand.

Scented pomanders like this one made from tiny dried rosebuds are ideal for scenting wardrobes and chests.

days when bowls of pot pourri looked like a pile of wood shavings; manufacturers are now concerned that the appearance of the ingredients should be in keeping with the character of the scent. As a result, pot pourri is liable to contain anything from seashells to pine cones, chunks of bark to dried berries. Although it does not last forever, pot pourri can generally be 'brought back to life' with a refresher oil. Even a small bowl of pot pourri placed on the hall table will have an instant and potent effect.

Light rings are another good way of allowing delicate fragrances to pervade your home. These are designed to sit on standard electric light bulbs and have a channelled groove running right round them into which concentrated oil is dropped. Heat from the light bulb evaporates the oil, gradually releasing its scent into the air. Although light rings are very effective, do be careful when using them as the oil becomes quite hot and may evaporate quickly. Make sure that the lamp is out of the way of small children and that the oil is never allowed to run dry in case it starts to burn.

Oil burners are another method of evaporating scented oils into the atmosphere. They come in two pieces – a small ventilated container to fit a night light or similar type of candle and a small dish or bowl which rests on top. The bowl is filled with some water and a few drops of oil are added. The heat from the candle burning below heats the water and evaporates the oil. Be careful that the water is never allowed to dry up as there is a risk of the oil burning.

Scented candles create a restful ambience both by casting a warm, flickering light and by releasing a subtle perfume.

Of course the most natural and still the best way of scenting your home is with fresh flowers and greenery. The very fact that the scent is transient will ensure that you enjoy it all the more. Flowers that are especially good for perfume include lilies, lilac, lavender, honeysuckle, pinks, wallflowers and stocks. While heavily perfumed, however, not all of these plants thrive as cut flowers indoors and may be best left out in the open air for everyone to enjoy. Lilies and roses generally do well indoors if their woody stems are split at the bottom and water is kept clean. If you are in doubt about the suitability of a flowering plant for longevity once cut, ask your local florist or garden centre.

Scented sachets have been used for hundreds of years to perfume homes and clothing. You can buy paper sachets ready-filled and perfumed, but simple muslin bags of rose petals or lavender look even prettier. Small bags may be tied around coat hangers to perfume your wardrobe while sachets and drawer liners bring a breath of fresh air to musty chests of drawers.

Room sprays shouldn't be confused with air fresheners which have an entirely different purpose. Room sprays are simply the quickest means of introducing scent to your home. They are not designed to disguise bad smells, though they may do so.

Flowers

Nothing can transform a room, even the dingiest and dullest room, like a bunch of flowers. Combining three potent elements – colour, shape and scent – they are an invaluable and instant way of cheering the saddest little corner.

These days the trend for formal floral arrangements is on the wane which is good news for anyone without the time or patience to perfect the art. With a general move towards simpler styles, flowers can look stunning even when displayed in the most casual way. There is no format for success when it comes to flowers but when working with natural elements like this, it's hard to go wrong. Take your inspiration from nature – look at the way colours work together and if you like something, try it at home.

If you aren't sure about the best way of combining colours, start off with varying

Glass vases in glowing jewel colours deserve the most lavish and showy flowers. With translucent containers, the stems become part of the arrangement.

shades of one colour. During spring and summer there's a wealth of fresh flowers around, so start by picking your favourite colour and take it from there. Posy-style arrangements are easy to begin with. Simply select flowers of a similar height and hue and gather them in a tight bunch. You can bind them with a length of raffia or narrow ribbon to keep them in shape.

Another idea for displaying blooms of a similar shade is to place them in a tightly grouped arrangement of containers, one for each variety of flower. This idea works best when the containers themselves have a common theme too – glass vases, blue and white china or lustreware, for example.

Sometimes unexpected planters can make almost as much of an impression as the flowers themselves. Bulbs are particularly adaptable – try planting single snowdrop or crocus bulbs in tiny flowerpots or make use of cracked and chipped crockery that no longer serves a useful purpose by planting a cup, jug or sugar bowl with spring bulbs. Place the planted china next to a few co-ordinating pieces such as plates and saucers to make a pretty, informal arrangement. Old tureens, vegetable dishes and even chamber pots all make suitable planters so look out for slightly damaged designs in junk shops and jumble sales. And redundant ceiling lights in the form of glass bowls look very effective when planted with ivy or other trailing plants.

While flowers are the stars of the show, greenery and other foliage plays an extremely important supporting role. You don't have to stick with Maidenhair fern or Eucalyptus; there are all sorts of other exciting possibilities which will liven up anything from a simple bunch of daisies to exotic arrangements of lilies. Try using stems of wheat or barley amongst autumnal arrangements or decorative grasses set amongst a posy of spring flowers. And if you are feeling adventurous, even vegetables can be used to great effect. Try working with unusual elements such as artichoke heads or decorative cabbages

which lend texture and bulk. Plain twigs, too, add interesting texture while shiny berries or bright red chillies add a magical touch to wintery bunches of dark green foliage.

Herbs can also be a tremendous source of decorative foliage. Rosemary has a silvery bloom and smells delightful, while lavender's sweetly scented purple blooms and delicately spiked leaves make it simply irresistible. Mint and sage come in many varieties, some of which have attractive variegated leaves. So the next time you visit your local garden centre, don't think of herbs in purely culinary terms!

Candles

Nothing beats candlelight for atmosphere. Whether you stick a stub of candle in an old bottle or unearth the family candelabra to illuminate formal dinner parties, the magical effect of softly flickering light will be the same. Candles provide a cheap and instant means of transforming any room – quite simply nothing beats them at creating mood lighting.

As the popularity of candles is on a steady increase, there has been a rush to come up with a host of inventive ideas for displaying and embellishing them. You can now buy a wonderful assortment of decorative accessories, some of which have a practical purpose too. There are tiny plate-like rings which slot over the candle to collect drips of wax at its base. Take this idea a step further and crystal drops are added which gives the effect of an ancient family chandelier – even if your 'heirloom' was bought at the high street sales!

Wall sconces, once the preserve of costume dramas, are now available in every shape and style conceivable. Add a touch of medieval melodrama to the plainest of metal candlesticks and sconces with gold or silver metallic tassels. Bought cheaply in haberdashery departments, they really do transform everyday items into glamorous artefacts. Another way of giving plain

LEFT *Wall-mounted wirework shelves like these allow you to display plants and flowers together in colourful rows.*

Beeswax and church candles glow warmly in a variety of candle-sticks, including well polished, carved wood and beaten pewter.

candlesticks a new lease of life is to twist lengths of ivy and other greenery around them. For special occasions you might like to spray evergreen foliage with gold, silver or bronze paint. And some intricate styles of candleholder may enable you to wire in blocks of oasis so that you can use fresh or dried flowers and berries as decoration. Of course the effect will be temporary, but it does mean that you can change the decoration to suit any occasion.

In days gone by, candles were often placed near mirrors so their light was reflected. This creates a magical atmosphere in large or small rooms with equal success. Another eye-catching means of reflecting candlelight is to incorporate the candle holders into the mirror itself. Although this idea is associated with a bygone age, there are reproductions of similar mirrors which cost just a fraction of the price of a genuine antique.

If you are keen to maintain symmetry, a candle at either end of the mantelpiece is a tried and tested arrangement. For a change, however, choose short ivory-coloured church candles and fix them into ordinary terracotta flowerpots (if they are old and weathered, so much the better). Make sure that the candles are secure before packing the base with sphagnum moss and tying a ribbon around the pot. Then arrange several of the 'potted' candles along the mantelpiece at regular intervals to provide a shelf of light. You can even buy tiny terracotta pots that are no more than a couple of inches high. Use the same idea for decorating them to use at place settings. Just make sure that the candles that you use are not too high for the size of the pot!

You can modify the decoration of the pots very easily. Try packing small nuts or pine cones around the candle base, or use dried flowers in small pieces of oasis wedged between the candle and the pot. Raffia or paper ribbon looks just as effective as expensive satin or velvet bows, so experiment until you come up with a look that you like.

Candle shades are perhaps the quickest way of transforming everyday candles into something special. Fixed to the candle by means of a brass carrier, shades add an air of occasion and the range of different styles offers tremendous scope. Choose from pretty pleated gingham shades for a cottagey look, or, for more formal rooms, shades in frosted glass or filigree metal. The cut-out design of filigree shades casts wonderfully atmospheric shadows but metal shades tend to be fairly pricey. If you are looking for a cheaper alternative, card shades with pinhole designs or tiny cut-out patterns work just as well.

If you wish, try painting your own design in watercolour or pen and ink on a plain shade. Another option is to cut single images such as flowers, cherubs or sun faces from wrapping paper and use them as decorative motifs. Simple ideas work just as well so if you don't feel like getting out a

Floating candles are ideal for creating a sense of occasion. A glass bowl with just a few floating candles makes a simple yet effective centrepiece for dining tables.

paintbrush, a gold felt tip pen 'scrawled' in a random pattern looks stunning against a dark background, or try tiny stars and moons cut from the card with a scalpel to act as windows through which the candlelight will shine.

Imagination is the only limit to the number of designs you can come up with. Just be sure that you never leave lit candles unattended – even for a moment – whether they have shades or not.

Candles have always been used at table centres but these days you don't have to rely on formal candelabra to create a stylish setting. There are bowls and baskets designed with candle holders around the edge. Pile them high with informal arrangements of fruit and leaves then light candles in co-ordinating colours to add the finishing touch. If you can't find bowls or baskets like those mentioned, you could secure candles in blocks of oasis or lumps of modelling clay and use them in conventional containers.

Of course, if you are short of time or don't feel creatively inclined, you could use candles that are designed specifically for special occasions. These come in every shape, size and colour imaginable and their real benefit is that they don't have to be displayed cleverly – their very design does all the work for you. Geometrically-shaped candles can look stunning in simple arrangements; spheres, pyramids and cones look equally effective whether used individually or placed together in groups. And because of their stable base, you don't need anything more than a plate to sit them on. Metallic candles reflect the candleglow and look especially effective on festive occasions such as anniversaries and Christmas. And for fun, there are candles cleverly shaped into a variety of novelty styles, from cakes and caskets to snowmen and angels. The trouble is that they tend to cost a lot – and usually look too good to burn!

Floating candles are a wonderful invention and are the simplest of all to display. A large glass bowl is all that's required – something around the size of a fruit or salad bowl is usually about right. The candles are quite small so they will not burn for a great length of time but will usually last as long as your guests! Some are shaped as flowers or have glitter added to catch the light but the plainest styles are very effective too. You might like to float fresh flowers with the candles or use individual candles in small glass bowls at place settings.

Lacquerware

Old storage tins and trays can be given a new lease of life with a coat of lacquer and a hand-painted design, inspired by floral-printed wrapping paper.

you will need

- Old tin or enamel kitchenware. Tin works best as you can give the surface a good key with rough sandpaper. Enamel may also be used but its surface is trickier to work on.
- Wet-and-dry sandpaper
- Lacquer undercoat
- High-gloss black lacquer paint
- Sky-blue and racing-green high gloss lacquer for the inside of the tin
- Small tins of lacquer paint in assorted colours appropriate for your chosen design

- 3cm (1 1/4in) decorator's brush
- Selection of artist's brushes for painting the design
- White spirit and jam jar for cleaning brushes
- Rubber gloves, rags and skewer for opening tins and stirring paint
- Mixing dishes
- Plastic sheet or newspaper for covering area
- Scissors, pencil, paper, tracing paper, metallic marker pen and masking tape

It takes nothing more than patience and a few pots of paint to turn old tinware into pretty, decorated containers like these.

step by step LACQUERWARE

1. Sand down the tin or tray with wet-and-dry sandpaper. To provide the surface with a really good key, it's worth taking time at this stage.

2. Apply two thin coats of undercoat to the inside and outside of the tin with a decorator's brush, allowing plenty of drying time between each application. Clean and dry the brush between each coat, ready for the next stage.

3. Apply two coats of coloured lacquer to the inside of the tin and lid, and then the handles, again allowing plenty of drying time.

4. Apply two coats of black lacquer to the outside of the tin and lid, using slow, firm brushstrokes to reduce the amount of bubbles appearing.

5. Measure the area on the tin to be decorated and choose a design to fit. Cut a large hole in a piece of white paper to the size of the decoration you require, move it over the design until you find a section with a good central feature. Stick the cut-out paper down on this section with masking tape.

6. Trace the main feature in the chosen area with pencil. Turn over the tracing paper and trace through on to spare paper, then position tracing paper 'original' right side up on your tin and set into place with masking tape. Trace through to the tin. You may find it helpful to use a metallic marker pen to clarify the outline at this stage.

7. Set out paints, brushes, white spirit and mixing saucers in front of the tin with the marked-up design. Starting with the darker background colours (here dark green and burgundy), paint within the traced areas, referring to the original design for guidance. Use the larger artist's brushes first to block in large areas of colour before progressing to more detailed sections. The smallest brushes should only be used for dots of colour here and there.

8. If you intend to use the newly-painted article, apply a coat of clear lacquer to protect the design and prevent it from chipping. Keep left-over paint for touching up scratches or any other damage.

STEP 1

STEP 2

Painted Pots

Add a splash of colour to patios and windowsills with colourful hand-painted flower pots. Look to the colours in your garden or the pages of magazines and books for inspiration. Start with bold patterns which are easiest to reproduce, then let your imagination run riot and add leaf and floral patterns or simple spots and stripes!

Plain terracotta pots have a smooth, porous surface which is ideal for painting and as they are inexpensive, it is not the end of the world if you make a mistake. Vinyl matt emulsion will provide good cover. You can buy small pots (or even match pots) of paint but you'll find that this is an excellent opportunity to use up small quantities of paint left-over from larger scale projects.

You will need soft brushes but don't buy anything too expensive as emulsion can be difficult to wash out. Try out different colour combinations and patterns on a scrap piece of paper or card before you start so that you are less likely to make major mistakes or feel dissatisfied with the end result. If you find that paint straight from the pot is difficult to work with due to its thick consistency, pour some into a separate container and thin it with some water

Give plain terracotta pots a Mediterranean look with brightly coloured paint brushed and scratched in bold patterns.

you will need

- Assorted plain terracotta pots
- Small, soft paintbrushes
- Vinyl matt emulsion paint

step by step PAINTED POTS

1. *Apply your base colour, doing several pots at a time as this will give the earliest pots time to dry while you work.*

2. *Gradually build up colours and patterns, cleaning brushes and allowing the pots to dry between each colour.*

3. *You can add extra decoration by drawing or scratching into wet areas of paint with the end of the brush or a pointed tool to show the colour or terracotta underneath.*

These pots will weather naturally if filled with compost or left outside. To avoid damp coming through and affecting the paint, line with plastic before potting and leave the base unpainted to allow moisture to escape.

STEP 2

STEP 3

Painted Throw

While Chapter 4 includes instructions for making a softly padded throw, you can make one that has quite a different look simply by using fabric paints. This plain length of peach cotton has been transformed with fruit and flowers painted around the edge to form a bright border.

Fabric dyes and paints are easy to use and come in an inspiring range of colours and finishes. With a little skill, you can transform an old sheet into a casual yet stylish throw like this.

you will need

- Length of plain cotton fabric, hemmed on all four sides
- Dressmaker's chalk
- Pieces of plastic sheeting
- Drawing pins and pencil
- Stencils or templates (optional)
- Fabric paints
- Paint brushes
- Iron
- Small piece of plain cotton fabric

step by step
THROW

1. *Drape the fabric over the sofa before painting to decide where you would like the designs to appear*

2. *Cover the table or worktop you will be working on with plastic sheeting. Pin the cotton fabric to the worktop with pins. Make sure the fabric is pulled taut.*

3. *Working on one area at a time and using a soft pencil, either draw a freehand design on the fabric or trace around stencils or templates.*

4. *Paint the design, building up the colours in layers. You must fix each layer of paint before starting another – when the paint has dried, place the small piece of cotton over the painted area and press with a hot iron. This fixes the paint and means the throw can be washed.*

Addresses

Anaglypta
Crown Berger
PO Box 37
Crown House
Hollins Road
Darwen
Lancashire BB3 0BG

Richard Burbidge Ltd
Whittington Road
Oswestry
Shropshire SY111HZ

Coloroll
Riverside Mills
Crawford Street
Nelson
Lancashire BB9 7QT

Crown Paints
PO Box 37
Crown House
Hollins Road
Darwen
Lancashire BB3 0BG

Dylon International
Worsley Bridge Road
Lower Sydenham
London SE26 5HD

Faber Blinds
Kilvey Road
Brackmills
Northampton NN4 0BP

Fablon
Cramlington
Northumberland NE23 8AQ

Fine Color
Green Hill Mill
Skipton Road
Colne
Lancashire BB8 0NX

Hamilton Acorn Ltd
Halford Road
Attleborough
Norfolk NR17 2HZ

Harrison Drape Ltd
Customer Services Dept
Bradford Street
Birmingham B12 0PE

H & R Johnson Tiles
Highgate Tile Works
Tunstall
Stoke on Trent ST6 4JX

Lakeland Plastics
Alexandra Buildings
Windermere
Cumbria LA23 1BQ

Arthur Sanderson & Sons Ltd
112–120 Brompton Road
London SW3 1JJ

The Stencil Library
Nesbitt Hill Head
Stamfordham
Northumberland NE18 0LG

Index

Acknowledgements

Page 10 Trevor Richards/HB; page 12 Roy Smith/HB; page 14 Spike Powell/HB;

page 15 Trevor Richards/HB; pages 16 and 17 Ian Kalinowski/HB; page 18 Tom Leighton/HB;

page 19 Brian Harrison/HB; page 22 Ian Parry/HB; page 22 Dominic Blackmore/HB;

pages 24 and 29 Trevor Richards/HB; page 31 The Stencil Library; pages 34 and 35 Crown Paints;

pages 36 and 37 Trevor Richards/HB; pages 39 and 40 Crown Paints; page 43 Hamilton Acorn;

page 44 Sanderson; page 46 CBT PR; page 48 Anaglypta; page 49 She/National Magazine Company;

page 54 Coloroll/Camron PR; page 55 Sanderson; page 56 Fablon;

page 57 Elizabeth Whiting Associates; page 58 Iain Bagwell/HB; pages 61 and 63 Trevor Richards/HB;

page 65 Spike Powell/HB; page 66 Faber PR; page 67 Ling Wong/HB; page 68 Derek Lomas/HB;

page 70 Ian Kalinowski/ HB; page 71 Harrison Drape; page 72 Trevor Richards/HB;

page 73 Ian Parry/HB; page 74 Brian Harrison/HB; page 76 Geoffrey Frosh/HB;

page 79 Trevor Richards/HB; page 80 Ian Kalinowski/HB; pages 82 and 86 Trevor Richards/HB;

page 88 Colin Poole/HB; pages 89, 90 and 92 Trevor Richards/HB; page 93 Richard Burbidge;

page 96 H & R Johnson; page 99 Sanderson; page 100 Trevor Richards/HB; page 104 Spike Powell/HB;

page 105 Ian Parry/HB; page 106 Ian Kalinowski/HB; page 107 Brian Harrison/HB;

page 108 Ian Kalinowski/HB; page 109 Marie Louise Avery/HB; page 110 Lakeland Plastics;

page 111 Graham Rose/HB; page 115 Peter Anderson/HB; page 118 Graham Goldwater/HB;

pages 119 and 120 Trevor Richards/HB; page 123 Dylon.